Korea: 1950–1953

by the same author

*

THE RED ARMY
THE RED ARMY OF CHINA
THE INDO-CHINA WAR, 1945–54
THE GREEK CIVIL WAR, 1944–49
MALAYA: THE COMMUNIST INSURGENT WAR, 1948–60
THE ALGERIAN INSURRECTION, 1954–62

Korea: 1950–1953

EDGAR O'BALLANCE

ARCHON BOOKS
Hamden, Connecticut

Contents

Maps

Preface

In this book I have attempted a review, in broad outline, of the war fought in Korea from June 1950 until July 1953. By now, the clouds of propaganda and emotional thinking that obscured it, not only while it was being fought but for a few years afterwards, have largely dispersed. Most if not all of the myths which surrounded it have been exposed for what they are. Moreover, a number of volumes of memoirs by people prominently engaged have appeared within the past few years; and these, when considered together, provide a fairly clear conspectus of the strategical thinking that lay behind the various campaigns of the war.

Usually described in present day military parlance as a 'limited war', although the limitations were completely one-sided, it was a vindication of the strategy of the nuclear deterrent. It was only when they thought atomic weapons were about to be used against them that the Communists concluded an armistice agreement. This fact is still not fully appreciated in the West.

It was a war in which a full-scale Chinese army clashed for the first time with a Western one; and the myth that the Chinese Communist soldier is able to march and fight indefinitely on a bandolier of rice was conclusively exposed. Large-scale fighting ceased when the Chinese People's Volunteer Army—unable to stand up to Western fire power—was beaten to a standstill within eight months of crossing the Yalu River. In the event, however, the Chinese Communists, in the 'negotiating war' fought at Panmunjom, very nearly succeeded in recovering all the ground they had lost in the 'shooting war'.

It was a war in which Communist psychological warfare techniques were seen in action and were proved generally to be effective. It was a war in which soldiers of many nations fought together for the first time under the banner of the United Nations; and it was a war bedevilled and complicated by power struggles between statesmen and generals, between statesmen and statesmen, and between generals and generals. In the end it provided a satisfying demonstration that, in democratic countries at least, generals, however headstrong and locally powerful, must not exceed the brief they have been given. It was, too—though here one is in the realm of hypothesis —a war in which, perhaps for the last time in history, nuclear weapons might have been used without the certainty—or, at any rate, without a very serious risk—of provoking a global conflict. And it was a war in which, quite clearly, the limitations of air power were exposed.

The war in Korea cannot be evaluated in isolation, but must be seen as a manifestation of the world-wide struggle between rival ideologies. The powerful Soviet Army was poised ready to move westwards into Europe; and it must be remembered that, three days after the Korean War started, the United States began a 24-hour alert by what became the Air Defence Command. Aircraft were continually in the air, ready for a war mission, with nuclear weapons on board. The North Atlantic Treaty had been signed in April 1949, a bare fourteen months previously, and efforts to persuade NATO countries to provide troops to fill out and strengthen this defensive shield were only partially successful. Fear of Soviet aggression was very real, and this round-the-clock alert has remained in operation ever since, although manned aircraft have given way to missiles. To some the war in Korea was fought in the 'wrong place, at the wrong time and against the wrong enemy', and was in effect an evasion of a confrontation with the real enemy, the Soviet Union.

This book does not purport to be a complete catalogue of every single action fought and I may be criticized, for example, for not covering in detail some of the prestige positional battles

that gained wide publicity in the last two years of the military
struggle when the front lines had stabilized. But too much detail
tends to obscure the outline, so I apologize if specific formations,
units, problems or actions in which individual readers may be
specially interested are not mentioned or commented upon fully.

In Korea I saw the fighting men of many nations in action
and their conduct would—if such a thing were possible—have
increased my already unbounded admiration for ordinary
soldiers of all nationalities. It was the actions of the military
and political leaders that—as so often before—puzzled and
saddened me.

EDGAR O'BALLANCE

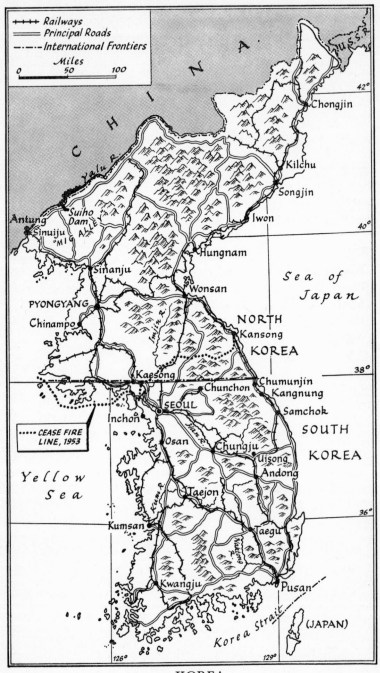

CHINA

U.S.S.R.

42°

Chongjin

Kilchu

Songjin

Yalu R.

Antung
Suiho Dam
Sinuiju "MIG"

Iwon

40°

Hungnam

Sinanju

Wonsan

Sea of Japan

PYONGYANG

NORTH

Chinampo

Kansong

KOREA

38°

Kaesong

Chunchon   Chumunjin
Kangnung

SEOUL

Inchon

Samchok

CEASE FIRE
LINE, 1953

Osan

Chungju

SOUTH

Uisong
Andong

KOREA

Yellow
Sea

Taejon

36°

Kumsan

Taegu

Kwangju

Pusan

(JAPAN)

Korea Strait

126°   129°

I. KOREA

Abbreviations

Sets of initials have been avoided as far as possible but a few are necessary for brevity. The most important ones are:

CIA   = Central Intelligence Agency
CICUNC = Commander-in-Chief, United Nations Command
CPVA   = Chinese People's Volunteer Army
KMAG   = Korean Military Advisory Group
KPA   = Korean People's Army
KATUSA = Korean Army Troops with the US Army
MLR   = Main Line of Resistance
ROK   = Republic of Korea
SKIG   = South Korean Interim Government
UN   = United Nations

CHAPTER 1

The Hermit Kingdom

The Korean War—in which the forces of the United Nations and of the Republic of Korea fought against those of the Korean and Chinese Communists who were aided by the Soviet Union—began on 25th June 1950, when North Korean troops invaded South Korea. On 27th July 1953, it ended in a frustrated stalemate when, after protracted delaying tactics by the Communists, an Armistice was finally signed. Beaten on the battlefield, they sought for many months to minimize their defeat by political, psychological and diplomatic means. The conflict was terminated only because the Communists became convinced that America had finally lost patience and was about to carry the war—perhaps with atomic weapons—to the Chinese mainland, which had been until then a secure sanctuary, arsenal, source of supply and reinforcements and a training ground for over one million Chinese soldiers south of the Yalu River.

Until the outbreak of war, so little was generally known about Korea that it was sometimes called the 'Hermit Kingdom'. A huge peninsula, varying between 90 and 200 miles in width and from 525 to 600 miles in length, it juts southwards from Manchuria; and it is strewn with jumbled mountains which are highest in the north, where some reach up to 8,500 feet or more. The broad main range, the Taebaek, runs down the east side of the peninsula, forming a natural barrier between the eastern and the western parts of the country.

Only 20 per cent of the land is arable and as a result intensive cultivation is practised, which occupies some 70 per cent of the population. Korea is, and always has been, a comparatively poor and technically backward country. Its people—some Confucianist, some Buddhist, some Animist, and some Christian —have been consistently exploited and oppressed.

A Chinese invasion about A.D. 100 established Chinese dominance over Korea. Buddhism reached the country in the fourth century, and this was followed later by Confucianism which had become generally accepted by the end of the thirteenth century. During the long period of Chinese suzerainty Korea enjoyed fairly complete autonomy.

In more modern times, lying as it did at a point where the ambitions of China, Russia and Japan met and conflicted, Korea became an attractive prize. To the north its frontier with Manchuria ran for 500 miles, and for an additional 11 miles with that of Russia, along the lower reaches of the Tumen River. To the west was the Yellow Sea, with the Shantung Peninsula only 125 miles distant, while to the south across the Korean Strait lay Japan, at its nearest point only 120 miles away.

The rising might of Japan faced the declining strengths of China and Russia, and one of the first moves in this power struggle was in 1876 when, in defiance of China, Japan forced a new trade treaty on Korea. It is worth remembering that this occurred only twenty-three years after Japan itself had been reluctantly prized open and compelled to enter the modern world—a dramatic demonstration of the explosive potential that had been released.

In 1894, Chinese troops were sent to Korea to assist the king in crushing a revolt. Japanese soldiers were also landed and the two invading forces clashed. In the course of an eight-month campaign the Chinese were completely defeated. The Japanese crossed the Yalu River, invaded Manchuria and took Port Arthur by assault. The Chinese sued for an armistice; and China had to cede Formosa, the Pescadores and the Liaotung Peninsula to Japan, and to recognize the 'full and complete independence of Korea'.

Ten years later, without the formality of declaring war, the

Japanese Imperial Navy attacked and destroyed the Russian Fleet in Far Eastern waters. A Japanese army landed in Korea and marched north to win the Battle of the Yalu River, before moving on to defeat the Czar's Far Eastern Army at Mukden. An Asian power had defeated a European one; Japanese prestige and influence became immense; and Japan's paramount influence in Korea, despite loud protests from Korean nationalists, was recognized by America.

In 1910, Korea was formally annexed by Japan, and it became known as the Chosun[1] Government-General. A period of colonial rule followed, during which the Japanese stifled nationalist aspirations. In 1942, when World War II was at a critical stage, Korea became an integral part of Japan, coming directly under its Home Ministry. Koreans were conscripted and used for second-line military duties such as guarding prisoners and acting as a labour force.

During this period, the Japanese modernized the country to some degree and introduced some industry. In the northern part where there were deposits of minerals such as coal, iron, tungsten, copper, graphite and gold, hydro-electric projects were established and dams constructed. The north, which contained large sections of forest, had a drier climate than the south, and its agricultural produce consisted mainly of wheat, millet, corn and soya beans, of which there was one crop a year. In the south, where most of the arable land had been cleared and was in full use—frequently terraced for conservation and maximum productivity—two crops of rice and barley were harvested annually. To a large extent the two parts of Korea complemented each other economically, and there was an exchange of rice,[2] barley, silk and textiles from the south for coal, wood and electric power from the north.

Covering an area of 8,500 square miles, communications were poor; only about 20,000 miles of roadways in the whole peninsula (in 1950) and some 3,500 miles of railway, much with limited carrying capacity. There was a shortage of rolling

[1] Chosun was the ancient name for Korea, meaning 'Land of the Morning Calm'.
[2] South Korea, for example, exported 100,000 tons of rice to Japan in 1950.

stock and trained personnel since, until 1945, the railways had been operated mainly with Japanese staff.

Despite repression, patriotic feelings remained alive; but active nationalists of all shades were either imprisoned or exiled. In March 1919, a spontaneous nationalist demonstration began in Seoul, spread to other parts of the country, but was eventually suppressed—and suppressed brutally—by the Japanese police. One of its most prominent leaders was Syngman Rhee,[1] who fled the country to form a Provisional Korean Government in Shanghai. He had protested when Japan annexed his country in 1910, but little notice was taken of him. Between the two world wars he lobbied his cause overseas, mainly in America, and in the process became the best known Korean nationalist leader in exile.

The Korean Communist Party was established in 1925, but was a feeble organization that ceased to operate three years later, although elements of it remained active. It was resurrected in the 1930s, but again did not prosper partly because of internal dissensions and partly because of efficient Japanese police action.

A Korean Communist who later came into prominence was Kim Il-sung,[2] a guerrilla leader who operated from just over the border in Manchuria; he caused some minor irritation to the Japanese security forces during the late 1930s. Reports of Kim Il-sung's activities and movements during this period are vague and conflicting. Some accounts, for example, indicate that he went to the Soviet Union in 1938, while others give the impression that he remained in the region of the northern frontier of Korea, fighting the Japanese security forces right up to 1941 or 1942. During this period there were numerous bandit political groups at large in the mountains of the north on both sides of the border, which gave vague allegiance to some left-wing, nationalist or anti-Japanese view, or at least gave lip

[1] Formerly Lee Sung-man.
[2] His real name was Kin Sung-chu. He adopted the name of a dead Korean resistance leader. He was reputed to have joined the Korean Communist Party in 1929—but this date is doubtful.

service to one as a popular and convenient cover for their own activities. There is no doubt, however, that at some date Kim Il-sung moved to the Soviet Union.

Little happened in Korea during World War II, though nationalists of various hues, and others at odds with the régime, escaped from the country whenever they could. Some went to the Soviet Union, which was not at war with Japan, and there Communists and other extreme left-wingers were welcomed, indoctrinated and organized. Others moved into Manchuria and through Japanese-occupied territory to reach the portions of north-west China held by Mao Tse-tung's guerrillas, where, once again, they received political and military training.

The tide of war turned in favour of the Allies, and at the Cairo Conference of December 1943, attended by Churchill, Roosevelt and Chiang Kai-shek, the subject of the post-war future of Korea was raised. Korea was promised eventual unity and independence. Further decisions taken at Potsdam by the Allied Powers in July 1945 confirmed the Cairo Declaration.

After Germany's defeat in the West, the war against Japan continued in the East. The Soviet Union was not yet involved, but was daily expected to march against Japan. As the end was in sight and in any case was no longer in doubt, American military planners, without consulting the Soviet Union, decided that the Soviet occupation forces should go into the northern part of Korea to receive the surrender of the Japanese, and those of America into the southern part. A demarcation line—which ran roughly, but not exactly, along the 38th Parallel—was drawn on a map, again without consulting the Soviet Union. The southern portion included two main ports, Pusan and Inchon, which the Americans would need to land their troops.

The first atomic bomb was dropped on Hiroshima on 6th August 1945 and two days later the Soviet Union hurriedly declared war on Japan. On the following day, the 9th, the second atomic bomb was dropped on Nagasaki. The Russians were only just in time. The formal date of the surrender was the

14th, when the fighting in World War II ended. By this time all four major powers, America, Britain, China and the Soviet Union, were openly committed to Korean independence.

Soviet troops crossed the northern border into Korea on the 12th and, moving quickly southwards, accepted the surrender of all Japanese forces until on the 28th they reached the 38th Parallel, where they halted. The Soviet Union in this instance respected the arbitrary demarcation line though it had not been initially consulted about its exact location.

The abrupt ending of World War II found American troops in the Pacific theatre widely dispersed and, owing to the huge distances involved, not easily available to land in Korea to accept the surrender of the Japanese in the southern part of the country. The Allies, it seems, were unprepared in other ways too and it was not until 2nd September that General Mac-Arthur, the Supreme Commander Allied Powers in the Far East, issued his now famous 'Order No. 1', instructing all Japanese armed forces in Korea north of the 38th Parallel[1] to surrender to the Soviet Army (which they had already done), and those south of it to surrender to the Americans.

The first US elements did not land at Inchon until 8th September, to receive the formal Japanese surrender at Seoul the following day. After this, US troops spread out to occupy the whole of Korea south of the parallel, which formed a boundary for this purpose that was respected both by the Russians and the Americans. But within days, as ideological differences became more openly apparent, the parallel became a barrier rather than a temporary boundary, on either side of which there emerged differing forms of government, based on opposing political beliefs and hostile to each other.

In the north, the Soviet authorities did not import a military government to administer the area temporarily until the antici-pated general elections were held throughout the whole of the country to elect a future government for Korea—as did the

---

[1] As a matter of interest, the 38th Parallel had been suggested as a dividing line between the Russians and the Japanese in the 1904-5 War, as it was something of a convenient strategic, even if not a sound tactical and economic, boundary.

Americans in their part—but instead governed directly through numerous People's Committees that sprang up in the Soviet zone, control of which was given to Soviet-sponsored Communists. Groups of Korean Communists who had been trained in the Soviet Union during World War II, and had returned with the Soviet forces, were used for this purpose, easily gaining ascendancy over the domestic Communists who were weak, divided and hardly organized at all.

In the first instance the Soviet authorities endorsed a popular local Communist as a figurehead over what was known as the 'Five Provinces Administration Bureau', but he was merely a stop-gap intended to gain local support. They had in fact brought with them a man they had shaped and moulded to their own specifications—Kim Il-sung, the old Korean guerrilla leader. He arrived in Soviet uniform, and was reputed to have fought at the Battle of Stalingrad. Under Soviet guidance and with Soviet assistance, Kim Il-sung assumed control of the *de facto* government of North Korea.

In December 1945, the 'Yenan' group, trained at Mao Tse-tung's headquarters in the North West Border Region, and later known as the Korean Independent Alliance, returned to Korea from China. Also, several thousand other Koreans who had been fighting with the Chinese Communists in various parts of North China and Manchuria, a great many of whom had received political as well as military training, came back to their homeland. Exiles, guerrillas, refugees, bandits and deserters from the Japanese Kwantung Army, they had formed the 'Korean Volunteer Corps' which had taken spasmodic part in guerrilla warfare on the side of the Chinese Communists against both the Japanese and the Chinese Nationalists.

There was suspicion and friction between the Yenan and the Soviet factions, but in July 1946 both were merged into the North Korean Workers' Party, which soon boasted a strength of 366,000. It maintained close ties with both the Soviet and the Chinese Communist Parties. Such small groups of nationalists as remained in North Korea were quickly eliminated by the Soviet authorities, and all permitted political organizations acquired a decisively Communist shape. Communist-type land reform was carried out in North Korea, and Communist ideology imposed on its people.

In an effort to find a solution involving a united, independent Korea, a Joint Commission, consisting of Soviet and American representatives, met at Seoul in March 1946, but a deadlock resulted. An interim trusteeship over the whole country for a period of years, as proposed by the major powers, was resented and rejected by Koreans from both north and south, since they all wanted immediate independence. Both, however, insisted on conditions that would ensure it was the type of independence they each individually wanted, but to which the other would not agree. After this each side pressed on with forming a government in accordance with its own ideological views.

In May 1947, the Joint Commission met again, made another attempt to find a solution, but again failed. This time the Americans suggested free elections for the whole of Korea, but the Soviet Union did not agree. Instead, it insisted on equal representation from both the north and the south in an Assembly, which the US rejected since the Communists might have been able to dominate it. The population of South Korea was about 20 million, and that of North Korea about 8 million.[1] As the situation was a stalemate, America passed the problem of uniting Korea to the United Nations, and in November the UN General Assembly set up a nine-nation Temporary Commission on Korea (UNTOK) to supervise elections. The Soviet authorities, however, refused to grant this Commission access to North Korea, and the deadlock persisted.

The Soviet authorities moved quickly and during 1946 all political parties in North Korea were merged and streamlined into the Korean National Democratic Front, and the country became a one-party state. The Provisional People's Republic had already been declared, and a Korean People's Assembly followed. During the next year (1947) the word 'provisional'

---

[1] Estimates of the population of Korea differ slightly, and some, for example, give that of North Korea as 10 million.

was dropped, and the country became the Korean People's Republic. In July of the following year the North Korean People's Council draft constitution was accepted, and the next month there were Communist-style elections to the Supreme People's Assembly. 8th September (1948) saw the appearance of the Democratic People's Republic, and two days later Kim Il-sung took office as Premier. By scheming, merger and purges in which rivals were removed, Kim Il-sung, aided by Soviet pressure and propaganda, had emerged as the unquestioned leader of North Korea. In this cut and thrust for power the Chinese-orientated Communists had been decisively out-generalled.

The South on the other hand, under an American military government, did not progress so fast towards Korean rule. Communism was firmly checked and a number of People's Committees, many Communist-led, that had sprung into existence before effective US occupation, were suppressed; but some Communist bandit groups, forced out of the cities, were active in the mountains of the interior.

In May 1947 the South Korean Interim Government (SKIG), dominated by a right-wing coalition led by Syngman Rhee, took office as a preparatory step to complete civilian government. Elections were held in South Korea under United Nations auspices, when 210 representatives were elected to the Assembly, 100 seats being kept vacant to be filled when elections were held in North Korea. A republican constitution was adopted and on 15th August 1948 the Republic of Korea (ROK) formally came into being, with Syngman Rhee as its President.[1] The US military government was terminated on that date, and one month afterwards the withdrawal of American Occupation Forces began. In December, the UN recognized the ROK Government as the lawful authority for the whole country, but in practice the Governments of North and South Korea each claimed jurisdiction over the whole of the country and declared the other to be illegal.

[1] For convenience the southern part of Korea will be referred to in the text as either South Korea or the ROK.

That month (December 1948) the Soviet Union announced that its occupying forces had completed their withdrawal from North Korea, and when the last American troops left South Korea in June 1949, the two parts of the divided country were left alone to face each other, which they did in an atmosphere of growing tension and hostility.

When the Soviet authorities entered Korea in 1945, they set up the nucleus of an armed force, known as the Peace Preservation Corps, which was composed in the first instance of trained Koreans brought back from the Soviet Union by Kim Il-sung. A few local Communists were enlisted, and their strength was boosted by the arrival of the Yenan group and other Koreans from China and Manchuria, until their total number eventually exceeded 18,000. The Peace Preservation Corps was armed first with Japanese weapons and later with Soviet ones. This force was additional to a smaller Border Constabulary and the usual Communist-type security police.

During 1946 and 1947 there was a fierce internal struggle in the Peace Preservation Corps for position and influence between those who had been in the Soviet Union during the war and those who had been in China. On its outcome depended the future shape, policy, arms and training of this force. The Yenan faction, under the influence of Mao Tse-tung, wanted a huge guerrilla-like army, consisting mainly of infantry and backed by militia; which meant that every man (and indeed woman too) would be a soldier, and a Communist soldier at that. The Soviet faction, influenced and conditioned by completely different war experiences, wanted a smaller, better equipped, better trained army, which would be a miniature copy of the Soviet one. Backed by Kim Il-sung, the pro-Soviet faction won and plans were made to build a small, mobile army on the Soviet pattern. Pro-Soviet personnel were placed in key positions and commands, and about 10,000 Koreans were sent off to the Soviet Union for specialist military training. A large Soviet Military Mission, amounting to over 3,000, came to North Korea, to establish training centres and to be instructors and advisers.

In February 1948, a Ministry of Defence was established, and the Peace Preservation Corps blossomed out into the Korean People's Army, the KPA, which expanded rapidly in strength as more combat-experienced Koreans returned home from China and conscription was introduced. The previous year (1947) for example, over 100,000 Koreans had been repatriated from Manchuria and many were instantly absorbed into the Peace Preservation Corps. When General Lin Piao's occupation of Manchuria was completed in 1948, the remainder of the Koreans serving with the Chinese Communist armies were allowed to return, and over 16,000 did so that year, most going into the KPA. Conscription came into force in July (1948) and several thousand young men, mainly on Communist political recommendations, were drafted into the KPA and the Border Constabulary. By June 1950, the overall strength of the KPA and the Border Constabulary amounted to over 135,000 all ranks.

During 1949, Soviet aircraft, tanks, weapons and equipment were sent to the KPA as fast as the returning Koreans, who had been trained in the Soviet Union, could absorb and handle them. This volume of modern material for the armed forces increased during the first half of 1950. In June of that year, the KPA consisted of seven full strength divisions, each with a few self-propelled guns and integral artillery, three under-strength ones, two independent regiments (one, for reconnaissance, equipped with motor cycles), and an armoured brigade. At full strength each division consisted of about 11,000 personnel, and had a triangular structure. The armoured force had about 240 armoured fighting vehicles, most of which were Soviet T-34 tanks. The KPA is estimated to have had over 2,000 guns of various types. All formations contained trained soldiers, and at least one-third had combat experience, mainly in China. They had been completely re-trained and re-equipped by the Soviet Military Mission. In addition, the Border Constabulary, more lightly armed and distributed in five brigades along the frontier region, had a strength of about 18,600. The North Korean Air Force had about 210 aircraft, including about 60 YAK trainers,

40 YAK fighters and 70 Ilyushin-10s. The North Korean Navy was equipped with 16 small patrol boats and a few coastal craft on which light guns were mounted.

The armed forces of South Korea made a much slower start, chiefly because the Americans thought that a small armed gendarmerie to maintain internal security would be enough. The Korean Constabulary, the nucleus of the South Korean Army, had a strength of only 5,000 in January 1947, but this was increased to around 15,000 during the year. When the hostile intentions and build up of the KPA could no longer be concealed this policy was hastily changed, and a belated expansion programme was embarked on. In August 1948, the Korean Constabulary became the ROK Army, and a US Korean Military Advisory Group (KMAG), of about 500 personnel, was appointed to give assistance. By January 1950, the ROK Army reached a strength of 60,000 and this swelled to 94,000 by June, organized principally in eight divisions. In addition, there were about 50,000 armed police. Though built up on the US pattern, the ROK Army was badly equipped; it had no tanks, no medium artillery, inadequate transport and it was short of ammunition. It had only 27 armoured cars, about 90 105-mm howitzers and just over 2,000 vehicles. Owing to the rapid expansion, less than two-thirds of its soldiers had completed their initial training, and many were raw recruits. The ROK Army lacked experienced officers, and in all respects it contrasted badly with that of North Korea. That month a defence agreement was made between the USA and South Korea, economic aid was given and more promised. The South Korean Air Force possessed 12 liaison and 10 trainer aircraft, while the Navy had only about 20 small coastal vessels.

Tension between the two states increased and there were several minor armed clashes along the 38th Parallel in which, on occasions, both were the aggressors. For example, artillery was used in the summer of 1949, but incidents along this uneasy frontier slackened off in May the following year. Neither country became a member of the United Nations as either America or the Soviet Union consistently blocked the application of one or the other. Both sides energetically used propaganda means to build up the tension between them.

In North Korea, within the Communist political organization now known as the Korean Labour Party, the Yenan faction, both political and military, had been defeated by the Soviet one and, through Kim Il-sung, Stalin called the tune.

In South Korea, Syngman Rhee was having internal Communist trouble. There was a serious military riot at Cheju in April 1948, and there were Communist-inspired mutinies in a regiment at Yosu in October and November, both of which were put down with severity. Over 2,000 Communists and suspected Communists were purged from the ROK forces after these incidents. At one time over one-quarter of South Korea was under martial law.

The North Korean Government claimed there were over 70,000 active Communists in South Korea, which was probably a fairly accurate estimate. In December Communism was outlawed, and the Communists had either to go underground or take to the mountains. The Communist bandit armed groups at large in the interior increased, and at least three out of the eight ROK divisions were engaged in dealing with them. Internal subversive elements and Communist-instigated espionage further reduced the efficiency of the ROK forces.

Despite the state of his armed forces and his Communist problems, Syngman Rhee was bellicose, and in February 1949 he declared that he could defeat North Korea in two weeks. Later, in October, he boasted he could take Pyongyang within three days. These words were provocative; and the authoritarian nature of his rule was causing concern amongst Western nations, and especially in America. The removal of the Allied Military Government had allowed Syngman Rhee to use his security police arbitrarily and to imprison many of his opponents. But although not liked by the American Government he was the only leader of any stature available and was backed for that very reason.

An opportune moment for Stalin to order the KPA to attack South Korea came in June 1950, when it was obviously much stronger than the ROK Army and should have been able to crush it quickly and without a great deal of trouble. Elsewhere in the world the situation was favourable to such an attempt. In Europe the Cold War was reaching a crescendo and only the American nuclear deterrent held back the Soviet armed forces. Stalin had no intention of engaging in an all-out war with the West and being attacked with atomic weapons, but he was determined to stir up a diversion in far away Korea. (Dean Acheson, the US Secretary of State, had publicly declared that Korea was beyond the American defence perimeter.) He wanted to test Western reaction to a small probing Communist attack and he may have thought that South Korea could be subdued before any effective military assistance arrived; and in any case he probably surmised that America would be afraid of starting a Third World War and would not intervene for this reason.

Stalin was not willing to enter any war in Korea openly, but he wanted to involve America as deeply as possible in Asia, and so restrict or drain off US aid to Europe which was bolstering up such countries as Greece and Turkey, and was thus thwarting his ambitions in that part of the world.

On the Chinese mainland the Communists, under the leadership of Mao Tse-tung, had just driven Chiang Kai-shek to take refuge in Formosa. Mao Tse-tung, who received no help at all from Stalin in his long struggle, rushed to Moscow where he spent ten weeks. While there, the outlines of Stalin's strategic plan to take over South Korea by force must have been discussed and finalized. Mao Tse-tung must certainly have been in favour of the North Koreans taking over South Korea as that would curb his old enemy, Japan, now resurgent, from expansionist adventures; and it would deflate US prestige in the Far East.

In the US Administration economy was the watchword and US military establishments and forces were running down rapidly, with further cuts in the offing. In broad terms American foreign policy was to contain the Soviet Union and its Far East basic military mission was to protect Japan against any sudden move by the USSR.

The North Korean Government felt secure, having friendly land frontiers to the north and west across which massive Communist aid could quickly be sent in an emergency. Confident and ready, the KPA waited for the signal to attack, and during the third week in June 1950, its divisions deployed to positions just north of the 38th Parallel.

CHAPTER 2

The Communists Attack

The Korean War began at 0400 hours[1] on Sunday, 25th June 1950 when, after a long co-ordinated artillery and mortar barrage at several points along the frontier, seven North Korean divisions, an armoured brigade and a mobile unit moved southwards across the 38th Parallel into South Korea. This force numbered about 90,000 men, and was initially accompanied by just over 100 tanks.

Tactical surprise was complete. Despite rumours that had been in circulation for months neither the ROK Government nor the USA had really believed that an attack would materialize that summer. The monsoon season had just begun and many South Korean troops were away from their units on leave. Reputedly a Soviet plan prepared by General Antonov of the Soviet Military Mission, the North Korean invasion straddled the country in five prongs. It was opposed by four ROK divisions and a brigade in defensive blocking positions just south of the Parallel, around Ongjin, Kaesong, Pochin, Chunchon and near the east coast.

The main thrust was down the traditional invasion route from the north, and one North Korean formation took Kaesong by 0930 hours. Just to the east, two divisions and most of the armoured brigade forced their way past Pochin, down the Uijongbu Corridor towards Seoul. To the west, two North Korean divisions moved south to the Ongjin Peninsula, to attack and cut off the one ROK division centred around

---

[1] Local time is quoted throughout, so technically it was 0200 hours (24th) in Washington, and 0700 hours (still the 24th) in London.

Ongjin. In the centre, two other North Korean divisions punched southwards towards Chunchon, while on the east coast units moved out to make two amphibious landings at Kangnung and Samchok, to combine with a land thrust down the coastal sector.

The first news of the invasion reached KMAG headquarters about 0900 hours, since a few American personnel with the ROK divisions on the Ongjin Peninsula were flown out to

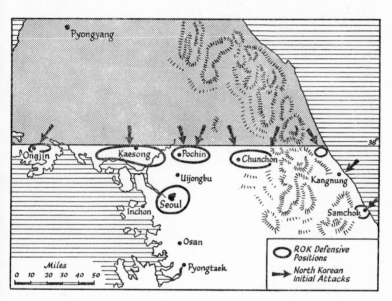

2. INITIAL THRUSTS OVER THE FRONTIER

Seoul to report back as soon as the first clashes occurred. At 1100 hours, the North Korean Government broadcast that it had declared war on the ROK because South Korean troops had invaded its territory. Consistent but sketchy reports of KPA forces biting deeper into South Korea which filtered back throughout the day left no doubt that this was a full-scale invasion and not just an over-sized border raid.

During the following day (the 26th) the invasion momentum carried North Korean troops further southwards and by evening the situation was causing serious alarm both in Seoul and

Washington, as it seemed that ROK forces were unable to offer serious resistance. President Truman ordered General MacArthur to intervene with US naval and air forces to evacuate American nationals, of whom there were about 500 in KMAG and another 1,500 civilians in South Korea, and another early American reaction was to send small quantities of military equipment from Japan to the ROK. Although Supreme Commander Allied Powers in the Far East, MacArthur was not responsible for the ROK Army or the defence of South Korea. President Truman ordered the US 7th Fleet which was in the area of the Philippines, about two days' sailing time away, to move to the Straits of Formosa, in case China tried to invade that island. The fleet was placed under MacArthur's command.

An emergency meeting of the UN Security Council was called, but no firm decisions were taken. However, the Council met again on the 27th and approved a recommendation that the United Nations furnish assistance to help the South Koreans (who were not members of UN) to repel aggression.[1] There has been and there still is some dispute about the legality and technical correctness of this resolution, but in any event the USA had a bi-lateral defence agreement with South Korea. The Soviet Union, which had boycotted the Security Council since January 1950, because Peking had not been given the Chinese UN seat, could have vetoed this resolution had its representative been present, but it is of academic interest only to speculate on what courses of action might have followed had this occurred.

Intensely preoccupied with the Cold War in Europe, President Truman was most reluctant to become additionally involved in a 'shooting war' in Asia. Only a few days earlier he had stated that the US would avoid further involvement in the Chinese Civil War. He hesitated, anxious lest that war should flare up again and involve the USA. There were divided views amongst senior American generals on the measures required;

[1] Of the 53 (out of then 59) UN members who approved this resolution, 40 eventually offered aid in one form or another, 16 sent armed forces and 5 sent medical units.

some believed that air and sea power alone could halt the Communist invasion, while others were sure that ground troops, and in large numbers, would be essential. The nearest US military ground formation, the 8th Army, engaged in occupation duties in Japan, consisted of four under-strength divisions.[1] And there were few armoured fighting vehicles in Japan at the time. Syngman Rhee asked for American help and on the 27th, when the evacuation of US nationals was in full progress, MacArthur was authorized to intervene with his naval and air forces to help the ROK Army. That day saw the first aerial actions of the war, when US Air Force planes shot down three North Korean aircraft near Inchon, and then four more later.

Having an overwhelming superiority in men and weapons, the KPA made good speed towards Seoul, its T-34 tanks[2] cutting their way through the surprised defenders who, having no anti-tank weapons to speak of, could do little to stop them. Some North Korean soldiers in civilian clothes moved forward to mingle with the refugees and, once behind the lines, donned uniforms and produced hidden weapons. Large tactical advantages were quickly gained. North Korean aircraft dropped leaflets (on the 27th) on the capital, urging surrender. This caused the ROK Government to evacuate to Taejon, and there was an exodus of a large part of the civilian population across the Han River south of the city. ROK troops also began to leave Seoul in haste, and a large bridge over the Han River, loaded with refugees, was prematurely blown long before North Korean forces approached. This meant that a mass of military equipment, including valuable transport and weapons, had to be left on the north side of the river. Many ROK soldiers crossed the river in boats in small groups, and on the afternoon of the 28th the KPA entered Seoul, meeting only scattered resistance. In this disaster it is thought that about one-third of all weapons and transport possessed by the ROK was lost or abandoned. The ROK Army seemed suddenly to fall to pieces,

[1] These were the 1st Cavalry, 7th Infantry, 24th Infantry and 25th Infantry Divisions, and each had only two (instead of three) regimental combat teams.

[2] Armed with an 85-mm gun, the T-34 weighed about 35 tons.

and a couple of days later there were only 50,000 or so of its troops south of the Han River, and only a couple of divisions and three or four regiments with any semblance of discipline. Over 40,000 South Korean soldiers were either missing, captured or dead.

On the 29th, General MacArthur flew over to Korea to find out for himself what the situation was. The scene was dispiriting: a broken, retreating army, forlornly pinning its hopes on the possibility of holding the line of the Han River against the invaders. MacArthur was of the opinion that this was feasible provided he could quickly bring in and use two of his four divisions from Japan. Although his air force was already striking at targets in North Korea, he had not yet received permission to employ US ground troops in the war. On the same day (29th) Chiang Kai-shek offered 33,000 combat troops to fight in Korea, but this was refused by President Truman, mainly because he thought it might antagonize China and reopen the civil war. MacArthur's reasons for recommending against acceptance, although the troops could have been ready to move within five days, were that they would have to be completely re-equipped and re-trained and would require US supplies and US supporting arms and services to keep them in battle. Also it would be illogical to send US warships to defend Formosa if a substantial part of Chiang Kai-shek's troops were elsewhere.

Apprehensive lest the appearance of US troops in Korea provoke World War III, President Truman still hesitated, and it was not until the day (the 29th) on which he received a note from the Soviet Union (in reply to one he had sent on the 27th), which he interpreted as meaning that the Soviet Union would not intervene in Korea against the US, that he authorized the use of American combat forces the next day. Even so, anxiety remained. Although it was thought that the Soviet Union would not send troops to fight in Korea, it might assist China to do so and a statement made in Peking about this time gave some colour to this possibility.

The situation was desperate and the decision to intervene came at the last possible moment. At once MacArthur ordered

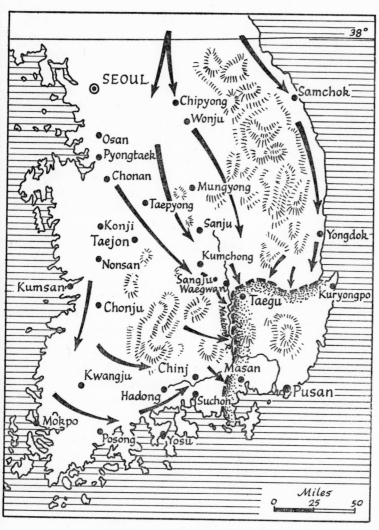

3. THE PUSAN PERIMETER

his 24th Infantry Division to be flown over from Japan, the first two companies, known as Smith Force,[1] arriving in Korea on 1st July. Landing at Pusan, Smith Force moved by rail to Taejon, and then by truck to take up positions on the north-south road, just north of Osan, about 25 miles south of the Han River. The remainder of the division followed, concentrating south of the Kum River, to form a block based on a triangle with points almost touching Taejon, Nonsan and Konji. On the 5th, North Korean tanks crashed into and cut through the northernmost US positions near the road. Armed with only a few 105-mm howitzers and some bazookas, Smith Force was unable to stop the T-34s, but it managed to account for at least four of them. Later that afternoon, Smith's men had to withdraw and scatter to the hills. The following day, North Korean forces with tanks leading smashed through another American blocking position near Pyongtaek, farther to the south, but other troops of 24th Infantry Division in the rear were able to slow the attackers down. Napalm was used[2] with some success against Communist armour by the US Air Force.

The US Far East Air Force, based mainly on Japan, but with elements at Okinawa, Guam and in the Philippines, had about 1,200 aircraft of different types at its disposal. This strength increased during the succeeding months. In addition, aircraft of the US Navy and the Marines, as well as light planes of the US Army, came into action on all fronts early in the war. For example, the three rail and one road bridge over the Han River had been destroyed by US aircraft in an attempt to hamper North Korean forces building up supplies on the south bank.

The momentum of the so-far victorious KPA began to slow down, and eventually beset by conventional problems of lack of fuel, ammunition and food, its progress came to a halt. But, although short of supplies, its main thrust could have exploited much farther forward against inadequate and hastily prepared defences. Instead, for about ten days there was what virtually amounted to a pause in the KPA offensive, during which T-34s

[1] Because it was commanded by Lieutenant-Colonel C. B. Smith.
[2] Napalm was reportedly first used on 30th June from 'jettisonable fuel tanks'.

and guns were ferried over the Han River, and North Korean divisions were redeployed across the breadth of the country. During this pause more US troops and equipment were brought into Korea, which enabled stiffer resistance to be put up when North Korean forces again advanced southwards. Undoubtedly, this was a critical moment of the war; had there been no pause, the KPA's chances of overrunning South Korea before substantial American military aid could arrive would have been very good. An opportunity for a swift Communist seizure of the whole of the Korean peninsula had been missed.

Material and military support from UN countries that had voted in favour of intervention was slow in forthcoming. Early in the field was Britain, which on 28th June placed warships in Japanese waters under UN command. The following day, Australia dispatched two warships and a squadron of aircraft to the battle area, and by this time Canada, New Zealand and the Netherlands were also sending, or preparing to send, naval forces to Korea. Other nations still hesitated.

On 2nd July, most of the torpedo boats of the small North Korean Navy were sunk or run aground near Chumunjin by a joint American-British naval force, and on the 4th, orders were issued for a complete blockade of Korea. B-29 aircraft (Superfortresses) from Okinawa bombed North Korean targets, while other American aircraft based in Japan engaged Communist planes in aerial combat until by 10th July UN air forces (as they can now be called) had complete aerial mastery. By the end of this month the North Korean Air Force had virtually ceased to exist and emphasis was switched to close ground support for the slowly retreating ROK and US forces.

On 8th July, General MacArthur, Supreme Commander Allied Powers in the Far East, was appointed Commander-in-Chief, UN Command (CICUNC), but it was not until the 14th that President Syngman Rhee formally placed all ROK forces under MacArthur's command. This was by letter, and was known as the Taejon Agreement, being made immediately before the ROK Army moved its GHQ from Taejon back to Taegu. Lieutenant-General Walton H. Walker, who had commanded the US 8th Army in Japan, was named Commander of all the ground forces fighting in Korea. He exercised command of the ROK Army through its Chief of Staff, but Syngman Rhee kept direct personal contact with its commanders, and on occasions issued instructions to them, often without the knowledge of the UN Commander.

After its brief pause for reorganization, refuelling and bringing up tanks and guns, the KPA resumed its advance, pressing hard against the ROK formations and the US 24th Infantry Division. The principal thrust was down the Seoul–Taejon railway line, but there was another powerful and almost parallel one to the east, aimed at Chipyong and Wonju, and the southernmost curve of the Han River. On the east coast yet another North Korean column was creeping southwards, having already reached Samchok. Although the invaders made advances on all sectors, it is notable that in places where they did not have armoured support the organized elements of ROK formations inflicted heavy casualties before being forced to give ground. Where tanks were used, as in the drive on Taejon, lack of anti-tank weapons prevented any really effective resistance from being offered. The central thrust, a strong one made with five North Korean divisions and an armoured unit, progressed well, reaching the Han River during the third week in July. From there the North Koreans fought their way up the watershed, through the passes in the mountains at Mungyong and Tanyang, and looked down the Naktong Valley to the immediate south.

On 9th July, US troops dropped back from Chonan and took up defensive positions just north of the Kum River, using the railway, now littered with derailed or damaged wagons, as its axis. The roads were strewn with abandoned equipment and trucks. On the 11th, US tanks, some M-24s, saw their first action in this war just to the north of the Kum River. The Communists pressed hard on the heels of the US soldiers, but the American division fought an effective delaying action just south of Konji, before retiring southwards across the Kum River. General Walker had hoped to hold the line of the Kum long enough to enable two more US divisions, the 25th Infantry (that had begun to arrive on the 10th) and the 1st Cavalry (that began to arrive on the 18th), to be deployed along the line of the Naktong River, where he thought he would be able at last to stop the Communist advance. Although US engineers blew the bridges over the river in this area the water subsided and the KPA was able to ford across in many places. This of course very seriously detracted from the river's defensive value, especially as the US formation on the south bank was thinly spread out. On the night of 13th/14th July, two KPA divisions crossed the Kum and enveloped US troops holding positions near Konji and Taepyong. The few tanks with the US troops were no match for the Communist T-34s. The 24th Infantry Division was forced backwards on Taejon, where it began to dig in. The US and ROK forces were additionally hampered with a refugee problem that hourly increased in seriousness. The North Korean security police, moving with the advanced elements of the KPA, ruthlessly shot many civilians. Rumours of this caused thousands to abandon their homes and flee before the advancing armies.

Soon Communist troops lapped against the outer defences of Taejon, and on the 19th they brought heavy shell fire to bear against the city, now mainly held by units of the US 24th Infantry Division. Over half a million refugees choked the streets, clogging defensive movements. That evening the attackers moved round the flanks, and next morning entered Taejon with T-34 tanks in the van. A number of new US 3.5-inch bazookas had been quickly flown in, but although in all they accounted for some 20 KPA tanks, the division was overrun and the city lost. Most of the survivors, including the commander,[1] took to the hills. This battle was a vital one, fought against heavy odds. Many US soldiers behaved very well, but some eyewitness reports tend to be critical of the behaviour of others. There was a spirit of hopelessness and confusion in the air which, together with the presence of

---

[1] Major-General William F. Dean, who after being in the mountains for about a month, was taken prisoner by the Communists.

demoralized ROK troops and panic-stricken refugees, must have created a black and defeatist atmosphere.

After the fall of Taejon on the 20th, it was a desperate race for space against time—for space on the part of the KPA, and for time on the part of the US and ROK forces. During the last week of July, US and ROK troops were pressed backwards into what became known as the Pusan Perimeter. But, even before that, certain flanking and threatening moves were made by North Korean formations in various parts of the country. On the east coast, for example, a KPA division was nearing Yongdok, only 90 miles north of Pusan. Before this, starting on 13th July, a North Korean division carried out a wide west-flanking movement from Kumsam, on the Kum River, through Chonju, and then westwards to Kwangju, elements splitting to clear Mokpo (on the coast), Posong, Suchon and Yosu. Concentrating at Suchon on 24th July, this KPA force presented a threat to the southern end of the perimeter, so the already battered US 24th Infantry Division was sent to intercept it. But American troops were ambushed near Hadong and the North Korean force broke through them to hit the Pusan Perimeter near Chinji on 1st August. The US division was ordered to hold the Masan sector. Farther north the US 1st Cavalry and the 25th Infantry Divisions were being pressed backwards to the Naktong.

On the same day (1st August), all ROK and US ground forces were ordered back into the Pusan Perimeter, which was to become a strongly held bridgehead. By this time US combat forces in Korea numbered about 47,000, containing elements of three divisions and a Marine brigade, while the ROK troops amounted to about 45,000, mainly remnants of former divisions and regiments, all under strength because of casualties. These forces were considerably handicapped by hordes of refugees, since the North Korean security police continued their policy of shooting anyone suspected of being anti-Communist or of aiding the Syngman Rhee Government. By the end of July it was thought that about 25,000 refugees were crossing the forward areas southwards daily, which hampered free movement and often masked fields of fire for the defenders. Also, many fifth columnists were infiltrated amongst the refugees. Ranged against the ROK and US forces were about 70,000 KPA soldiers, now re-formed into ten infantry and one armoured division. In the fierce fighting that had taken place on several fronts, the ROK troops had given a good account of themselves when equally matched, and this was borne out by the fact that the KPA had suffered about 58,000 casualties,[1] a far greater number than was estimated at the time.

On 4th August, all bridges on the approaches to the Pusan Perimeter, which extended about 80 miles from north to south, and 50 miles from east to west, were blown and the battles for the bridgehead commenced. US reinforcements and material were pouring into Korea through the port of Pusan in a desperate race to strengthen the defences before the Communists attacked in force. Three weeks of confused struggle began. Although the KPA was controlled by Kim Il-sung from his Supreme Headquarters, the perimeter battles about to start were directed by General Kim Chaek, who set up a Front Headquarters at Kumchong. The US 8th Army GHQ was at Taegu.

On 7th August, the US 24th Infantry Division attempted a counter-attack from the Masan sector, but it had indifferent success, and although it caused many North Korean casualties, it did not succeed in drawing KPA formations from other sectors of the perimeter. This movement had to be terminated on the 14th, since a dangerous situation was developing to the north where, between the 5th and the 8th, five KPA divisions and an armoured formation had forced themselves across the Naktong River with the intention of taking Taegu. The advance was held, although ground had to be given up in the process. On the 19th, a counter-attack drove most of the North Korean troops back over the Naktong. Meanwhile, the ROK Government moved to Pusan. In the north-east a North Korean division had reached Yongdok by the 5th, trapping a ROK

[1] The US estimate at the time was that the KPA had only suffered about 31,000 casualties by the beginning of August 1950.

formation which had to be evacuated by sea. After this a small counter-amphibious landing was made on the east coast near Kuryongpo.

Generally, by 20th August, the main fighting had run down on all fronts, although a series of combats involving tanks continued in the area of the road from Sangju to Taegu. US forces were receiving a few M-26 (Pershing) and M-4 (Sherman) tanks,[1] which were better able to hit back at the T-34s. These small battles subsided by the 25th. During this fighting, on the 16th, the first huge 'saturation' raid by heavy bombers was made on North Korean assembly areas. Others followed, but they failed to make the KPA relax its pressure on the perimeter. Doubts about the value of saturation bombing, which had been so effective in certain circumstances in the latter stages of World War II, and which had so many forceful advocates amongst the American generals and military planners, began to be expressed. During the retreat to the Pusan Perimeter the air forces had concentrated upon close support to the troops on the ground but, once the perimeter defences hardened towards the middle of August, the emphasis was largely switched to interdiction of North Korean supply lines. There seems in fact little doubt that the saturation raids did contribute substantially to slowing down the KPA momentum. Obviously the first task of the air forces was to establish control of the air space over their own territory, which was accomplished during the first month of the war. The second task, that of the destruction of enemy aircraft and of gaining control of enemy air space, was more than partly completed: and the UN air forces were able to carry out strategic bombing to destroy targets in North Korea, such as oil refineries, manufacturing complexes and communications centres, and to retard supplies to the Communist army in the field. During August napalm was used more intensively against enemy vehicles.

A comparative lull in the fighting followed which lasted for about ten days, during which both sides brought up reinforce-

[1] The M-26s (Pershings), weighed 43 tons and mounted a 90-mm gun, while the M-4s (Shermans) weighed 37 tons and had a 76-mm gun.

ments, fuel, ammunition and other supplies, and as far as they could, reconstructed their formations. Amongst the first UN reinforcements was the British 27th Infantry Brigade,[1] consisting of about 2,000 all ranks, which arrived in late August. Tanks and vehicles were also landed in Korea in numbers, until by the end of that month the US forces had over 500 M-26s and M-4s, as against the 100 or so T-34s which it was estimated was all the KPA had left in running order.

The UN ground strength rose to about 180,000,[2] but in that figure was counted some 92,000 ROK troops, of which a proportion were in labour units. In August, General MacArthur approved plans to integrate up to 100 ROK personnel into each company-sized US unit (Marines excepted). They were only partly trained, but they filled the ranks as infantry soldiers and they were known as KATUSAs (Korean Troops with the US Army). Their toughness, local knowledge and keenness made them welcome assets to US formations that had a manpower shortage in their combat squads. The strength of the KPA rose to about 98,000 men: 13 infantry divisions, a depleted armoured division and two small armoured brigades. Arbitrary and prompt conscription enabled these formations to be kept up to strength.

On the night of 31st August/1st September, the KPA opened an offensive against the Pusan Perimeter, making several co-ordinated attacks at various points. The Communist troops broke through in a number of places, but everywhere were unable to exploit their limited success. On the 5th (September) the re-named 27th British Commonwealth Brigade was committed to action, its task being to hold a sector of the perimeter near Waegwan. The KPA was short of fuel, ammunition and food. Despite the UN interdiction raids, enough got through to

---

[1] 27th Infantry Brigade contained the 1st Battalion, The Middlesex Regiment and the 1st Battalion, The Argyll and Sutherland Highlanders. On 3rd September, the 3rd Battalion, Royal Australian Regiment arrived and joined this Brigade, which was renamed the 27th British Commonwealth Brigade.

[2] Although not technically correct, for convenience, when UN forces are mentioned as such, this will automatically include ROK personnel as well unless otherwise stated.

enable it to continue to exist, but not enough to enable it to mount a large offensive successfully. The KPA conscripted thousands of locals to carry supplies forward at night. As bombing did not seem to halt the enemy, a switch was made to tactical close air support which proved extremely effective and was a main factor in this week-long battle. By the 7th, the KPA offensive was spent; the defences of the Pusan Perimeter had held and the Communist attack had been defeated.

A brief retrospect. During the first disastrous phase of the war, complete surprise enabled the stronger and better equipped KPA to cross the 38th Parallel and drive the ROK Army southwards. After a few days' fighting, the South Korean forces were in poor shape and only prompt action on the part of the US prevented their complete collapse at an early stage. US and UN authority enabled General MacArthur first to use his air forces and navy to evacuate American nationals, then to bomb strategic targets and give close support to the tottering ROK Army, and finally to land and use US troops, which were later joined by a small British formation. When the initial reluctance of the American Government to intervene directly was overcome, American resources, such as the 8th Army, the 7th Fleet and the Far East Air Force, were quickly deployed and brought into action.

After the fall of Seoul, the pause while the KPA brought its tanks and guns over the Han River enabled the first US division to reach the front. US troops, intervening in the midst of a retreat, slowed down the KPA advance and boosted ROK morale. Another KPA pause, mainly caused by supply shortages, enabled the Pusan Perimeter to be strengthened. The unsuccessful KPA offensive during the first week in September showed its limitations and demonstrated that the UN defences were in fact too strong for it to overcome. The North Koreans had anticipated a two-month campaign, and the fighting had already outlasted that period. Their army was gasping at the end of a long, vulnerable and tenuous supply line.

The UN air forces, predominantly American, had been particularly active, but had changed their strategy several times. There were conflicting schools of thought, some feeling that heavy strategic and interdiction bombing was the best solution, while others were of the view that tactical close ground support was the only answer. The result was that both methods were tried and each proved effective in its own way. The strategic and interdiction bombing greatly reduced the volume of Communist supplies, thus strangling the major September offensive, while tactical air support was of immense value to the ground forces, both in the withdrawal to, and in defence of, the perimeter. Although UN forces had been driven back and compressed into a comparatively small space, control of the air and sea enabled men and material to pour into Korea so that the initial adverse ratio of strength began to tilt in favour of the UN.

Meanwhile General MacArthur was planning boldly to end the war in the grand manner. He visualized a large amphibious landing in the rear of the enemy to trap the KPA in a vice and destroy it. But he was working against diverse and often hostile factions and personalities. US defence policy was hesitant and uncertain. For reasons of budgetary economy the Defense Secretary, Louis Johnson, had ordered cuts in the armed forces and in military expenditure generally. He was reluctant to change this and provide extra men to fight in Korea and the extra material required to back them up. Johnson was at loggerheads with the US Secretary of State, Dean Acheson, who was also against stepping up the war in Korea, but for a different reason. Acheson did not want the Chinese civil war to erupt afresh, as he feared America might become deeply involved. He had firm views on the line America should pursue in the Far East. Both men and their respective policies were unpopular with the US Joint Chiefs of Staff in Washington and with the military hierarchy as a whole.

It was barely a year (October 1949) since Mao Tse-tung had proclaimed his Chinese People's Republic in Peking, and in America public opinion had scarcely got used to the loss of China to Communism and to the discrediting of Chiang Kai-shek whom it had supported for so long. Chagrin and disillusionment, coupled with apprehension about the strength of the Soviet Union and of Stalin's intentions, reduced US policy on the Far East to a state of complete indecision. At first all open support and most financial aid to Chiang Kai-shek were hastily withdrawn, and then on second thoughts they were partially restored, when it was felt that the loss of Formosa might be yet another heavy blow to American prestige. In early August, President Truman authorized extensive military aid for the Nationalist Chinese forces on Formosa, and General MacArthur was instructed to carry out a survey to find out exactly what it would be best to send.

MacArthur, much of whose career and experience had been in the Pacific theatre, had decided opinions on the value of Formosa and he emphasized its strategic importance. He personally disliked the US policy of giving it such a low defence priority, and never made any secret of the fact that he thought the main Communist military threat lay in Asia rather than Europe. It was almost fourteen years since MacArthur had been home to the USA, having continually refused invitations to return even for short periods for conferences or consultations, and his opponents alleged that he was out of touch both with current American military thinking and with American public opinion. Many felt that he was not fully aware of the menacing reality of the Soviet Union. On 31st July he had visited Formosa for talks with Chiang Kai-shek. Nothing firm resulted from this meeting, which was probably an exploratory and liaison one, but it caused anxiety in Washington, especially as MacArthur appeared to sympathize with Chiang Kai-shek's plan for developing Formosa into a spring-board for the launching of an eventual invasion of the Chinese mainland. President Truman sent an emissary to insist that MacArthur should not behave like this again without instructions from Washington; he was told that he must not station any US fighter aircraft on or send any US ground forces to Formosa without the explicit permission of the Joint Chiefs of Staff.

Already UN policy in Korea, which was really US policy vaguely affected by British and other UN interests, appeared makeshift, uncertainly wobbling along from day to day, with an underlying tug-of-war in progress between the Commander-in-Chief on the spot and the authorities in Washington.

On 12th September, Louis Johnson resigned and General Marshall was appointed Secretary for Defense in his place. General Marshall, the author of the Marshall Plan to rehabilitate a devastated Europe, had been sent by Truman to China in 1945 to try and bring about unification. He failed, but the knowledge he had acquired of the Chinese Communists caused him to side with Truman and Acheson in giving greater priority to Europe than to the Far East. Marshall was thought to be one of those who favoured a more moderate approach to China and he was unsympathetic to MacArthur's ideas. There was an overall reluctance in the Pentagon, as well as on the part of the US Administration as a whole, to send anything to the Far East that might weaken America in its attitude towards the Soviet Union.

MacArthur wanted an all-out naval blockade of the Chinese mainland, but this was not agreed to. Britain and other UN countries were not in favour of such a drastic move, partly because it was too provocative and partly because a degree of commerce was developing with China which they wished to foster. Britain and France were anxious also in case the USA should be persuaded to abandon its European commitments to concentrate its strength in the Asian theatre. It was not until early August that MacArthur was allowed to undertake aerial reconnaissance flights along the coast of the Chinese mainland.

CHAPTER 3

Advance to the Yalu

MacArthur went ahead with plans for an assault landing at the port of Inchon, on the west coast, which was miles behind the KPA forward areas and close to its main supply routes. From Inchon he could move quickly inland and seize lightly held Seoul to form an 'anvil' against which UN troops moving northwards from the Pusan Perimeter would drive the KPA. He was informed that a Marine division could be assembled and brought into action in Korea by mid-September; in Japan the US 7th Infantry Division was being reinforced, equipped and made ready for battle. He decided therefore to use these two divisions as the core of an amphibious force that was to be filled out with ROK units. In the Pusan Perimeter the arrival of reinforcements and supplies enabled the defences to be strengthened and made it feasible to mount an offensive at the same time.

During the planning stage MacArthur ran into opposition from many quarters, including the Joint Chiefs of Staff in Washington, the Navy, his own staff officers and other experts, and also from the commander of the Marine division that was to spearhead the assault. The main Joint Chiefs of Staff objection was to his dividing his forces in the face of the enemy, and also because a Marine brigade would have to be withdrawn from the Pusan Perimeter, where it had recently arrived,[1] to complete the Marine Division earmarked for the assault on Inchon. The removal of a brigade would, it was argued,

[1] The 1st Provisional Marine Brigade had started landing in Korea on 2nd August.

48

seriously weaken the Pusan Perimeter defences, which might
have to withstand extra pressure while the amphibious operation was in progress. The loss of the Pusan Perimeter would be
disastrous, and would not be compensated for by a foothold at
Inchon, as in such an eventuality the bulk of the KPA could be
quickly turned against any UN troops landed there. Technical
objections were made by the Navy to the choice of Inchon as a

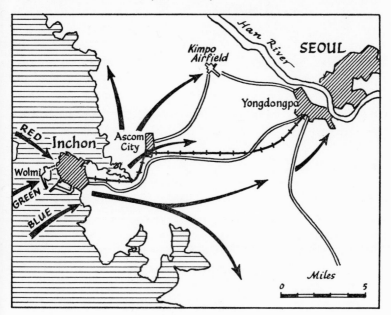

4. THE INCHON LANDING

site for an amphibious operation. The main one was that there
was a deep tide, which only allowed a short period twice daily
when assault craft could get close in to the shore. The tides on
the west coast rose up to 33 feet, while those on the east coast
were as low as three feet. Also, the rivers in the Inchon area
empty into flat basins that become broad estuaries where at low
tide up to five miles of soft mud flats are exposed which would
make any stranded ships or landing craft a sitting target for any
shore batteries. As a bridgehead port, Inchon's harbour and
other facilities were poor. Moreover, there was an island,

D 49

Wolmi,[1] dominating the approaches to the harbour, that would have to be dealt with first and separately, which would cancel out any element of surprise. It was pointed out, too, that landing in the heart of a city meant there would be no fields of fire for the assaulting troops, who might well become involved in slow and laborious house-to-house fighting. Indeed there was a danger that the whole invasion force might become hopelessly bogged down in the port area, and be totally unable to exploit the landing. The coastline of the peninsula was about 6,000 miles long, and there were at least eight other major ports in Communist hands, many smaller ones and numerous good off-shore anchorages. Other possible landing places were suggested, but MacArthur insisted on Inchon. Reluctantly, permission was given for the project, known as Operation Chromite, and troops were loaded on to ships that set off on various dates, according to their speeds and locations, towards Inchon.

'D' Day was set for 15th September, when there would be a maximum depth of 31 feet of water at high tide at Inchon, which was considered to be just sufficient. The two US forma-tions, the Marine Division and the 7th Infantry Division, together with a ROK Marine element and supporting troops, became known as X Corps, which was placed under the com-mand of Major-General Edward M. Almond. The remaining UN ground troops in Korea were known as the 8th Army, and were commanded by General Walker.

MacArthur boarded the *Mount McKinley*, which joined the converging convoys. Obtaining the use of, and assembling, some 260 ships of several nations, and of loading troops and equipment on board them, had been a triumph of military skill, staff work and intrigue on the part of MacArthur and his staff. The ships, American, British, Australian, New Zealand, French and Dutch, carried about 70,000 personnel. The leading ships appeared off Inchon early on 15th September, and after it had been bombed and pounded with rockets, at 0630 hours US Marines landed on the island of Wolmi (known as Green Beach

[1] Often written as Wolmi-do. As 'do' merely means island, this will be omitted.

for this operation), which had already been subjected to aerial bombardment for the previous five days. Only a few scattered shots were fired by the dazed defenders at the assaulting troops, who by 0800 hours had completely occupied the island for the loss of only one man killed. The Marines remained in position while the deep tide ebbed and flowed. During the afternoon (of the 15th) covering fire from the ships was directed on to the city, and two landings by Marines took place at about 1730 hours. One was on the northern edge of Inchon (known as Red Beach), and the other just to the south (known as Blue Beach). Within six hours the Marines were firmly in possession of the port and by dawn (the 16th) they had expelled all KPA elements from the city. The Marine Division, which had with it four battalions of South Korean Marines, then moved eastwards towards Seoul, which was held by one North Korean division. One group entered the industrial suburb of Yongdongpo, on the south bank of the Han River opposite the capital, while another moved north-east to seize Kimpo airfield, the largest in the country. The airfield was secured on the 17th, and the Marine Division at once moved in to take Seoul. On the 18th, the US 7th Infantry Division, which contained about 8,000 integrated ROK soldiers (or KATUSAs) in its ranks was landed, and at once moved southwards to Suwon, which it seized on the 22nd. Meanwhile the battle for Seoul raged, and it was taken by the Marines on the 26th,[1] after some hard fighting. UN casualties in the Inchon landing and the fighting for Seoul and Suwon were estimated to be about 3,500. Those of the Communists were probably more than twice that number.

The 8th Army now had four corps, the ROK I and II Corps along the north side of the perimeter, the US I Corps on the Taegu front and the US IX Corps along the Naktong River. To be the 'hammer' to the 'anvil', General Walker was instructed to mount an offensive from the Pusan Perimeter against the restraining forces, which he began on the 16th in the north-west sector. This offensive immediately ran into determined resistance, and his troops did not cross the Naktong River until the

[1] The fall of Seoul had been prematurely announced on the 25th.

19th, a fact which caused MacArthur some anxiety since he wanted to take Seoul before it could be reinforced.

Next day the Communist defences were being steadily penetrated and abruptly, on the 22nd, North Korean forces containing the 8th Army in the Pusan Perimeter began to withdraw, evaporating into the hills to the north and west. So suddenly and completely did this happen that it must have been the result of an order to move rapidly back, perhaps to help to defend Seoul, but more probably to extricate as much of the KPA force as possible before it was trapped and completely destroyed. There is no doubt that MacArthur's landing at Inchon was the major cause of this withdrawal, rather than pressure from the 8th Army. Many North Korean soldiers changed into civilian clothes and mingled with refugees, while others escaped northwards. Some units remained intact and fought well until scattered by superior UN firepower.

On the 23rd, the US 1st Cavalry Division began moving to the north-west, meeting little resistance, until it eventually made contact with troops of the US 7th Infantry Division, near Osan, on the 26th. At the same time the US 24th Infantry Division raced towards Taejon, while the recently arrived US 2nd Infantry Division, and the US 25th Infantry Division, moved towards the west coast, clearing the country as they advanced. ROK divisions moved northwards along the east coast, the eastern and the central mountain chains; and they marched with, and spread out behind, the advancing US formations. Many North Korean divisions had simply disintegrated and the UN troops[1] cast a wide net in an attempt to catch as many KPA prisoners as possible. Many thousands were captured but thousands of others slipped across the 38th Parallel.

The US Psychological Warfare Branch sprang into activity and, by radio and by leaflets dropped from aircraft, rammed home the hopelessness of the KPA position, urging its soldiers to surrender and guaranteeing them humane treatment. How

---

[1] Becoming more truly a UN force, as it was joined in the field at the end of September by a Philippine battalion.

much this contributed to the sudden withdrawal cannot be assessed, but many North Korean soldiers who surrendered said they were influenced to some degree by these psychological methods.

With the KPA ejected from South Korean territory, the military task was completed, or so it seemed, and on 29th September, General MacArthur formally handed control of the country back to the civil government of President Syngman Rhee at a ceremony at Seoul. This act did not endear him to his critics, many of whom thought that this was a political matter which he should not have taken upon himself, and that he did it for personal prestige reasons. Another reason why handing back power to Syngman Rhee rankled with many in America was the authoritarian nature of the ROK régime and the fact that security police executed without trial many Communists and people suspected of helping or collaborating with the North Koreans. Only after protests in America and Europe had these summary killings been stopped. However, as UN forces moved northwards to reoccupy South Korea, overwhelming and damning evidence of murders and atrocities perpetrated by the North Koreans came to light. Many mass graves were unearthed, and in Taejon, for example, about 6,000 bodies of civilians killed by Communists were discovered. A later provisional UN report estimated that about 26,000 South Koreans had been liquidated during the brief Communist occupation. These disclosures did much to neutralize objections to Syngman Rhee's methods of governing.

The KPA as a fighting army had been virtually destroyed,[1] and UN troops met little resistance in taking physical possession of the whole of South Korea. It is thought that between 25,000 and 30,000 North Korean soldiers—no more—managed to get back across their own frontier, mostly as individuals or in small disorganized groups. Thousands of KPA personnel wandered vaguely northwards, many of whom were eventually captured or gave themselves up. Figures released in November 1950 claim that the UN forces held about 135,000 North Korean

[1] General Ridgway in his *The Korean War* tends to differ from this conclusion.

prisoners, and had in addition inflicted some 150,000 casualties. It is believed that at its peak the KPA, with auxiliaries, numbered about 325,000, but over half this number must have been hastily conscripted men, of whom many had probably served with the KPA only for a few days, perhaps as porters or labourers.

The next problem, a political one, was whether or not to pursue the remnants of the KPA over the 38th Parallel and destroy them completely; and by occupying North Korea to unite the country. MacArthur was in favour of taking full advantage of the favourable military situation, but the Joint Chiefs of Staff, in Washington, were doubtful and hesitant. Eventually they passed the responsibility for making this decision to MacArthur, to whom they gave a Directive (on 27th September) to destroy the KPA, and, if it was necessary for this purpose, to cross the frontier into North Korea. How else could he have wiped out the KPA under the circumstances is hard to see. A proviso was included in the directive that MacArthur could only move north if there were no indications that either Soviet or Chinese forces were moving, or about to move, into North Korea. Also, he must not cross the Yalu River; and he was to use only ROK formations in areas adjacent to the frontiers with China and the Soviet Union.

MacArthur, too, was under pressure by Syngman Rhee, who was in no doubt at all about whether or not the frontier should be crossed. He had always taken the view that his Government was the only legal one for the whole of Korea, and had already said (on the 19th) that it was his intention to pursue North Korean troops over the border. He gave orders to certain ROK formations to move northwards, two of which in the east crossed the 38th Parallel on 1st October. Another ROK division moved through Seoul, making for Pyongyang, the North Korean capital. Once ROK units were in fact inside North Korea, MacArthur no longer had any cause to hold back UN troops and he planned to move the 8th Army on a broad front over the 38th Parallel as far as Pyongyang.

The first US troops, elements of the 1st Cavalry Division,

crossed the frontier on 9th October,[1] and were soon in the van of the advance, meeting only spasmodic hit-and-run resistance as they advanced. US units halted south of the line of Pyong-yang–Wonsan. MacArthur ignored the instructions from the Chiefs of Staff and used US and British troops in places to spearhead the movement northwards. He had little confidence in ROK units at this stage, considering them to be too much of a risk, owing to the inexperience of their officers and general lack of technical knowledge and training. In this advance the main problem was not enemy activity, but lack of fuel and food as units outran their supply columns. MacArthur decided to move X Corps, which remained separate from, and was not under command of, the 8th Army, by sea to positions on the east coast of Korea round the southern tip of the peninsula. (The exception was one Marine brigade that went by road to Pusan, to be picked up there by ships.) His object was to capture the iron and steel mills, power plants and port installations of north-east Korea before they were sabotaged or badly damaged.

Greatly taken with the idea of a united Korea under UN auspices, the UN created, on 7th October, the Interim Committee of the UN Commission for the Unification and Rehabilitation of Korea. On the 9th, MacArthur issued an unconditional surrender demand stating that unless the North Korean Government capitulated, he would take the necessary action to enforce the UN decree for unification, and three days later (on the 12th) the UN Committee advised MacArthur to take over the civil government of North Korea for the time being. The war seemed to be over.

In this triumphant phase of the Korean War, from a position of desperate weakness MacArthur, in the space of three weeks, had turned the tables completely and snatched a spectacular victory. His amphibious landing at Inchon had succeeded, Seoul had been taken, the KPA had been cut off and pressure on the Pusan Perimeter released. Defeated and broken, the KPA had withdrawn, losing thousands of prisoners and suffering

---

[1] Some reports indicate a day or so earlier.

many casualties. ROK units had swept across the 38th Parallel and UN formations had followed although they had generally halted along the line of Pyongyang and Wonan.

This success had hinged on the Inchon landing, and it was only when it was examined in retrospect that it was realized what a hair-raising gamble it had been. Military logic, science and calculation had all been against it. The narrow margin between victory and failure frightened the Pentagon planners and the risks taken sobered even the most enthusiastic. To quote two examples—a fault in the Communist intelligence network and a delayed mine-laying programme were advantages that played luckily and unexpectedly into UN hands. Had there been no such fault—or no such delay—the outcome might have been very different. The assembly of an armada of ships and some 70,000 men took time and could not be completely concealed. Communist agents were aware of the operation, its objective and, a few days before it took place, even its date, but for some reason this intelligence was not passed back in time to Kim Il-sung at his Supreme Headquarters. Had he known of the pending assault he could have reinforced Inchon and organized effective defences. Again, the landing forestalled by a few hours mine-laying in the Inchon harbour approaches, which had been unexpectedly delayed. If it had been carried out as planned, it might have wrecked the entire operation.

CHAPTER 4

Communist China

In the spring and summer of 1950 Communist China had many internal problems—some very pressing indeed—and was in no shape to engage in war with a major power such as America. Apart from devastation by years of war and a ruined economy, the previous year had brought many natural disasters—floods, famine, drought and disease. About 40 per cent of the budget was still allocated to military purposes and this was a heavy burden, when money and manpower were so urgently required for rehabilitation. The Government had a vast guerrilla problem on its hands, and at least one million soldiers (of a five million strong army) were fully engaged on 'bandit suppression' in the interior. There were still at large many thousands of Nationalist guerrillas, dispossessed landlords, political dissidents and plain bandits, especially in central and southern China, who were all actively antagonistic to the new Communist Government for their own several reasons. Mao Tse-tung admitted (in 1950) that there were at least 400,000 'bandits' to be dealt with. In late 1952 it was stated by Po I-po, the Minister of Finance, that two million 'bandits' had been liquidated in the preceding three years.

Apart from hard-core Communist formations, the Army itself might have been unreliable had it come to fighting either against the Nationalists or even the Americans, as nearly one-third of its personnel consisted of former Nationalist soldiers. If the situation were to have changed many, in the old Chinese tradition, might easily have turned their coats again. Another third consisted of hastily recruited peasants, whose main desire was to get back to their own plot of land as soon as possible, and who at this stage had been barely touched by Communist indoctrination. Large though the Chinese Army was, it was poorly equipped; the only arms it possessed were those taken from the Japanese on their surrender after World War II and those captured from the Nationalists. There was no air force; few tanks; only a handful of miscellaneous guns and little motor transport. No Soviet munitions had yet been sent to China.

As well as Formosa, many off-shore islands—some very close indeed to the mainland—were held by the Nationalists, and the Chinese Army had not shown up well in attempts to occupy them. In October 1949, for example, an amphibious assault on Kinmen (Quemoy) had been beaten off, during which Chinese troops suffered heavy casualties. This caused a pause in off-shore operations and it was not until April (1950) that the 4th Field Army was able to occupy Hainan. The 3rd Field Army had settled mainly in Central China near the coast, with the task of seizing many of the Nationalist-occupied off-shore islands. In February (1950) an epidemic ravaged this formation and thousands died since the medical services were very primitive. Morale declined and it was not until May that the Army had recovered sufficiently to seize the Chusan Islands, near Shanghai.

Its next—and major—task was to invade Formosa. Amphibious craft were assembled and training began. It had been hoped to co-ordinate the invasion with a political rising on Formosa itself, but in the spring (1950) this plan was uncovered, and Chiang Kai-shek destroyed the plotters. This indicated that there would be strong opposition and the 3rd Field Army began to prepare for a hard fight. The operation against Formosa seems to have been planned for the end of June, and between the 10th and 24th of that month Chinese troops on the mainland opposite were increased in number from about 40,000 to over 156,000. Although scheduled, the invasion of Tibet had not yet started and probably awaited the successful occupation of Formosa.

Meanwhile another gigantic troop deployment was slowly taking place. The 4th Field Army, which had a total strength of over 400,000 which had marched and fought from Manchuria through China, and which had finally captured Hainan Island, was ordered to return home. At least half the men were Manchurians, the others being added during the trek southwards. This move began in April (1950), and by July large numbers had returned. Owing to lack of roads and transport, troop movement in China was ponderous and slow, the men having to march on foot for most of the way.

The Chinese reaction to the North Korean invasion of South Korea was quiet and cautious, and the news was not released to the public until two days later. While in no way responsible for this invasion, the Chinese Government probably had prior knowledge of what was going to happen and Mao Tse-tung may have discussed the situation with Stalin while in Moscow. The rulers of China did not want war with America: they had enough problems of their own to cope with. But they did see that the pattern of world power was changing, great nations were declining, empires were breaking up and colonial territories were gaining independence. Nationalists in the Dutch East Indies were fighting a successful insurrectionary war, and the Greek Communists a less successful one. There was a reasonable likelihood that South Korea could be taken over quickly without unduly serious repercussions.

However, in China some precautionary measures were taken. The projected invasion of Formosa was called off in view of the move of the US 7th Fleet to the Straits. Certain troop deployments took place; in particular, about 30,000 soldiers from the 3rd Field Army, stationed opposite Formosa, were moved north to join about the same number from the 4th Field Army, in Shantung. From this mid-way position, they could be sent either to reinforce Manchuria, or moved back to take part in the Formosan operation if it were decided, after all, to embark on it. There were no other moves or open preparations for active intervention in Korea. Nor did this seem to be a probability, as Mao Tse-tung's strategic doctrine, based on the use of superior numbers in a mobile role, with guerrillas operating among a friendly peasantry, would hardly have found the narrow Korean peninsula an ideal field of operations. China watched during the initial retreat of the ROK forces and the UN intervention, but made no move, except to rouse public opinion against the Americans. Diplomatically, China spoke on the side of the Communists but unvociferously. The chief propagandist for the Communists on the world forum at this stage was the Soviet Union.

For a while it seemed as though China was content to stand by and watch the Korean War being fought out on its doorstep, despite UN intervention, but in the latter part of August there was a sudden change of attitude. In that month there were high-level conferences between the Chinese and the Soviet Governments, at which China was obviously persuaded to take an active part in the war. No details of these negotiations have been released and one can only surmise about what passed, but it was probably confirmed that the Soviet Union would supply the arms and China the manpower. Soviet arms, aircraft and vehicles were dispatched to China, and Chinese troops began to move towards the frontier with North Korea. Several thousand Koreans serving with the Chinese Communist forces were released and sent, complete in their units, to North Korea, causing General MacArthur to allege on 18th September (three days aft.r the Inchon landing) that China had given substantial help to the Communist forces in Korea by the transfer of combat-experienced troops. It has been suggested that this decision to intervene with troops was taken by the Chinese Government only because it was sure that America would not make aerial attacks on its territory, even though its soldiers might be fighting US forces in Korea, and that this information came from Western security leaks. Also, China may have been persuaded by the Soviet Union that America's supply of atomic bombs was small and its means of delivery weak. Now that the Soviet Union had developed a similar weapon the inference might be that such atomic weapons as the USA had would be held for use against that state rather than against the huge square mileage of China.

While Chinese troops were marching towards Korea, preparations were being made on the diplomatic side to justify intervention and to give some warning of intention. On 20th August, Chou En-lai sent a cable to the UN expressing concern over the Korean problem, and other protests of a gradually hardening nature followed. One alleged that, on 7th August, US aircraft had flown over the Yalu River, machine-gunning the airfield at Antung and the railhead at Talitzu. America offered to pay compensation, provided the damage could be inspected, but China did not respond. China also accused American aircraft of firing on Chinese rivercraft on the Yalu River, but there was no reply from the US. On 30th September (the day before ROK troops crossed the 38th Parallel), Chou En-lai gave warning in a speech that China would not tolerate aggression on a neighbour. The following day he formally notified Panikkar, the Indian Ambassador to Peking who had set himself up as an unofficial intermediary, that if American soldiers moved north over the Parallel, China would intervene in the war. Nothing could have been clearer; but this warning was not taken seriously at General MacArthur's Headquarters or indeed by any of the UN nations involved in Korea. On the same day (the 2nd), Vyshinsky, the Soviet Foreign Minister, made proposals for a cease-fire in Korea. The conditions were virtually impossible, but it began to seem as though the attitudes of the two major Communist Powers had been reversed—China was threatening, while the Soviet Union was in favour of negotiation. Three days after UN troops crossed the 38th Parallel a Chinese spokesman again warned that the Chinese people would not stand by if there were an American invasion, but little notice seems to have been taken.

Even if China's decision to intervene in the war in Korea had not been taken already (one feels that it had, although there was still time to retract if necessary), it was certainly made when UN troops moved northwards into North Korea. By this time air raid shelters were being constructed in Mukden and other major cities in Manchuria, air defence drill was being practised and massive troop concentrations were forming just north of the Yalu River.

Despite the clear warnings issued by China, the signs were not read accurately by Western statesmen, many of whom felt either that the country had too many internal problems to cope with to be able to indulge in war, or that it was still possible to isolate it from the Soviet Union. Some thought that an ideological split between the two huge Communist Republics might occur, on the lines of the then current Tito-Stalin dispute. Britain, for example, although it had soldiers fighting in Korea, had offered to recognize the Peking régime in January (1950). The offer had been refused because Britain would not support Communist China's claim to the Chinese UN seat, and also because of differences over Hong Kong. In America, Acheson represented a section of opinion that felt the revolution was more Chinese than Marxist and that Mao Tse-tung was a nationalist and a neutralist, rather than an international Communist. Hints were dropped that, once the Korean problem was solved, Formosa might be allowed to fall into Chinese Communist hands and that a friendly relationship could then begin. Acheson was convinced that China and the Soviet Union were already in disagreement over frontier territories, and he and President Truman were sure that Mao Tse-tung's Government could be influenced by an attitude of good will. The general view in America seemed to be that China was unlikely, in her desperate economic plight, to intervene at this stage in Korea, especially since a couple of divisions if used a few weeks earlier could have swung the balance and won the war. Why should China intervene now, when the UN forces in Korea were so much stronger?

There were strong pressures in America, and also in the UN, to unite Korea by force, but President Truman was cautious and wanted to be certain that China would not be provoked into active intervention. It would be a great advantage, he decided, to meet General MacArthur to discuss the situation at first hand; and the two men met, for the first time, on Wake Island in the Pacific on 15th October. It was thought by some to be a political manoeuvre and that Truman was trading on MacArthur's popularity after the Inchon victory to gain an advantage for his own party, the Democrats. The meeting was heavy with mutual suspicion. Truman tried to impress upon MacArthur that Chinese Communism could not be overcome by force, and that at this juncture Europe was a far more dangerous area than the Pacific. He was anxious over the Soviet Union's attitude and intentions, and stressed the need to avoid incidents with Soviet forces or on Soviet territory. On 9th October two American F-80s (Shooting Stars) had shot up a Soviet airfield near Vladivostok, some 60 miles inside the Soviet border. He insisted that such an incident must not be allowed to happen again. MacArthur stated that the war in Korea was almost over, that he did not think China would intervene, and that he would soon be able to release a division for the European theatre. A week or so previously (7th October) the invasion of Tibet had begun, which MacArthur estimated would keep the Chinese army fully occupied. MacArthur's military assessment was that there were about 300,000 Chinese soldiers in Manchuria, of whom probably not more than 100,000 or 125,000 were distributed along the Yalu River. He thought that only between 50,000 and 60,000 could be moved across the Yalu bridges; and that since the US Air Force had bases in Korea, and the Chinese no air force at all, if these troops made for Pyongyang, they would be exterminated.[1] There was a correct but stilted atmosphere between the two men at this meeting, at which there seems to have been a wealth of unspoken disagreement. MacArthur left on the 16th, as soon as he could, to fly back to Korea. He had under-estimated the President. Truman was unhappy about Mac-Arthur's attitude towards the Administration's policy and said later that MacArthur had misled him over China's intentions.

[1] There 'would be the greatest slaughter' were the reported words.

CHAPTER 5

China Enters the War

MacArthur returned from his meeting with Truman still convinced that China would not openly enter the war, so he set about occupying the whole of Korea at once and raised the restraining line for UN troops—which had been temporarily fixed as running across the peninsula from just north of Pyongyang–Wonsan—to one that ran roughly from Sinanju to Hungnam. On 19th October, advancing ROK and US troops, after some fighting, took Pyongyang, the North Korean capital, and ROK troops looted it. On the 21st, the Communist radio announced that the North Korean Government had moved to Sinuiju, on the Yalu River. North Korean personnel were surrendering in thousands.

There seemed no longer to be any reason to hold back forces impatient to reach the Yalu River and so complete the occupation of the country, and, on the 24th MacArthur abolished the restraining line completely. Already, on the 8th Army front, a race for the frontier had begun on 20th October. A regimental combat team of paratroops had been dropped near Anju, about 40 miles north of Pyongyang, in an attempt to rescue some UN prisoners and to cut off retreating Communists, but it failed to achieve its object. American soldiers moved forward carelessly and there was an 'end of the war' atmosphere. Many threw away their heavy ammunition, grenades and steel helmets as they motored almost casually northwards. Everyone was sure the campaign would be finished before winter set in.

While the 8th Army was advancing in the west, X Corps was sailing up the east coast, the Marine Division making for

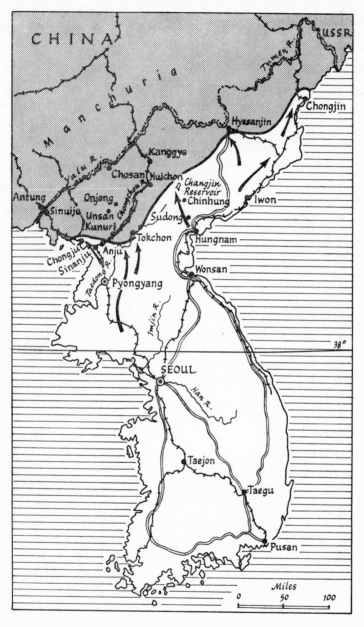

5. THE LIMITS OF THE UN ADVANCE

Wonsan, which it reached on the 20th, only to find that ROK troops moving on land had forestalled it, arriving on the 10th. As the harbour approaches were mined the Marines had to stay on board until the 26th. When they disembarked, elements set out northwards in the direction of Kanggye. The 7th Infantry Division arrived at the port of Iwon on the 29th, and on landing moved northwards towards Hyesanjin, on the Yalu River, while ROK formations under X Corps command, that had also disembarked at Iwon, moved along the coast towards Chongjin. The decision to move to the Yalu River did not please the Joint Chiefs of Staff in Washington, but MacArthur justified it on the grounds that the North Korean forces were weak and badly led, and that this was the opportune moment to deal with them. There had been differences of opinion between MacArthur and the Joint Chiefs of Staff since crossing the 38th Parallel as to how far the UN forces should advance into North Korea.

Advancing northwards from Pyongyang, leading elements of ROK formations on the right flank of the 8th Army ran into the last thing they expected—Chinese troops in strength. Already, on the 23rd, nine Chinese soldiers had given themselves up to a ROK unit, saying they were Nationalist Chinese co-opted into the Communist army, who had been forced to 'volunteer' to fight in Korea. Since they were thought to be subversive agents, their story was not believed. On the 26th, the leading battalion of a ROK division reached the Yalu River near Chosan. The next day it was ambushed and wiped out by Chinese troops. During the following two days the remainder of the ROK division was attacked and destroyed in the area of Huichon and Onjong. A ROK division near Kojang in the same region was surrounded and forced to scatter, while another withdrew after contact with Chinese formations. A flanking ROK division fell back, leaving the right side of the 8th Army gaping open. On 2nd November, a US Combat Team was decimated by Communist forces in the Unsan Valley, an incident that marked the end of the UN forward movement.

Although there was no further aggressive activity on the part of the Chinese troops in the west, in a fog of uncertainty and confusion 8th Army units dropped back to the line of the Chongchon River. The intelligence services had failed, and no one knew exactly what was happening. It seemed certain that Chinese soldiers had entered the fray, but as some reports indicated they wore North Korean uniforms it was unclear whether they were 'volunteers', stiffening the North Korean formations, or whether they were complete units from the regular Chinese Army. The fact was that the Chinese regular army, under the guise of 'volunteers', was in fact intervening in the Korean War on a massive scale. The Chinese Communist armed forces, later known officially as the Chinese People's Volunteer Army (the CPVA), under the veteran PLA[1] Commander, General Lin Piao, started—probably on 14th October (although some reports indicate a day earlier)—to seep quietly across the half-dozen bridges over the Yalu River into North Korea, and to deploy for battle. Moving only at night and hiding by day, they had escaped detection by UN reconnaissance aircraft. Between 14th October and 1st November, about 200,000 Chinese troops from the 3rd and 4th Field Armies moved silently into Korea[2] and by the latter date vehicles and guns were being moved over the bridges. The CPVA was formed into 'armies', which can be roughly equated to a Western corps formation, but without the conventional infrastructure and supporting arms and services. Each of these 'armies' was made up of either three or four divisions. The divisions, having an average strength of about 10,000, were triangular, with three regiments and an artillery unit. The build up of the CPVA was pushed forward at great speed but secretly; and it was later estimated that by mid-November there were between 270,000 and 340,000 Chinese troops south of the Yalu River.

To the east, ROK soldiers of X Corps reached the Changjin Reservoir by 27th October, to be fired on by the CPVA, which was deploying in that region. On 2nd November a Marine

---

[1] People's Liberation Army of China.
[2] The reported figures vary between 180,000 and 228,000.

regiment arrived, and for the next five days fought a series of engagements with the Chinese in the Sudong–Chinhung area. The CPVA suffered heavy casualties from UN fire and eventually withdrew. There was a general flurry of contacts between forward elements of the UN forces and the CPVA, and MacArthur (on the 6th) listed six such incidents—but there were in fact more. On 7th November the CPVA broke off action all along the front and it was obviously not prepared to become involved before it was absolutely ready. On that date, China admitted that Chinese 'volunteers' had been 'in action in Korea' since 25th October.[1]

On 6th November, MacArthur gave orders to destroy the bridges over the Yalu River, but this was countermanded by the Joint Chiefs of Staff in Washington, no doubt on political instructions, and all UN air strikes within five miles of the frontier were forbidden. MacArthur eventually managed to get this decision reversed but by the time the US Air Force attacked the bridges it was much too late, since over 200,000 Chinese soldiers had already crossed them, together with quantities of stores, guns and vehicles. In any event, the river froze over in mid-November and was no longer a barrier to infantrymen.

Because of faulty intelligence work,[2] MacArthur did not correctly appreciate the situation and failed to realize that his deduction that China would not enter the war was wrong. He thought the Chinese troops in Korea were part of a small token force that had been sent as a gesture from a neighbouring Communist country, and might be merely a screen behind which the KPA could recuperate. Nevertheless, he asked (on 7th November) for permission to bomb bases and concentration areas just north of the Yalu River, but this was refused. A few days later, on the 15th, it was reported that a Soviet diplomat had said that if UN aircraft attacked Manchurian airfields, the

[1] It had been admitted in Peking on 2nd November that Chinese 'volunteers' were in Korea.

[2] General Ridgway seems to be of the opinion that faulty interpretation of the available intelligence reports (*The Korean War*) was the source of the trouble, and there may well have been some substance in this on occasions.

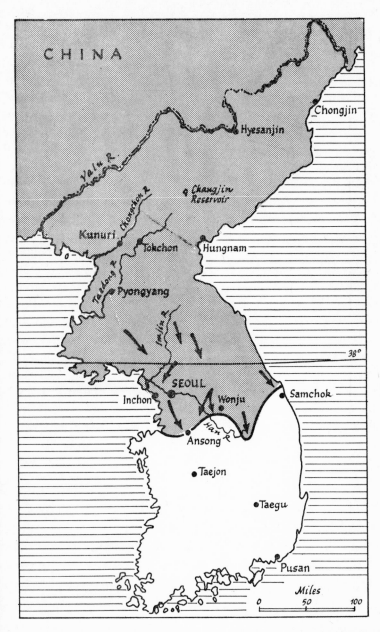

6. THE LIMIT OF INITIAL CHINESE ADVANCES

Soviet Union would strike back. No doubt this did much to influence both Truman and the Joint Chiefs of Staff in constantly withholding permission to bomb targets north of the Yalu. MacArthur's instructions were to occupy the whole of Korea so that the country could be prepared for elections under UN auspices, and as he was under the impression there were only about 60,000 Chinese soldiers there he did not anticipate any substantial difficulty in accomplishing his mission. The fact that the CPVA was deliberately quiet for about a fortnight while it was making its own final preparations, strengthened his view.

Another fact which should have been an additional warning was the appearance of Chinese air power. According to intelligence reports, China had no air force at all for practical purposes, and that of North Korea had been destroyed, leaving the skies over Korea completely free to UN aircraft. But Communist MiG-15s appeared in the sky over the Yalu on 1st November. They kept clear of UN fighter aircraft, and it was assumed they were flown by Soviet pilots. Daily more were seen, and the first jet aircraft combat in history took place on the 8th, when a US F-80 (Shooting Star) brought down a MiG-15, flown by a Chinese pilot, over the Sinuiju area. It was suddenly apparent that a Chinese air force was being built up with Soviet assistance and modern Soviet machines, and was concentrating in bases north of the Yalu River, such as Antung, which were just out of the destructive reach of UN aircraft. Permission for 'hot pursuit' of Communist aircraft by UN fighters over the Yalu River was firmly withheld.

General MacArthur planned an offensive, due to commence on 24th November (the day after American Thanksgiving Day) aimed at sweeping to the frontier and clearing all Communist troops from Korea. By now winter had set in and the UN forces had no heavy clothing. There was an air of hesitation and reluctance among the UN troops—a 'Home by Christmas' feeling—rather than a determination to pursue the war. It was alleged that General MacArthur had said that this offensive would end the war and had told his commanders to tell their soldiers they would be home by the New Year. Later, this was officially denied by him, and he claimed his words had been misinterpreted. Nevertheless, a certain amount of damage had been done by this rumour to UN morale. The 8th Army contained four US divisions, the ROK II Corps, which also consisted of four divisions, and other UN troops, including the 27th British Commonwealth Brigade and the Turkish Brigade.[1] General Walker, its commander, started to line them up along the Chongchon River in preparation for a general advance on a wide front. Opposing the 8th Army were at least 16 Communist divisions. Separated by a gap of about 75 miles, to the east was X Corps, consisting of three US divisions, two ROK divisions, and other troops which included a British Marine Commando Group. When it had completed the occupation of north-east Korea, X Corps was to swing left and make an enveloping movement to assist the 8th Army. Opposing it were at least 14 divisions from the 3rd Field Army. In all about 300,000 CPVA troops faced about 440,000 UN soldiers, the latter having superior arms and firepower.

On 24th November, 8th Army troops moved north along parallel roads, and the next day at some points ran head-on into the CPVA, which was commencing a major push southwards. One of the first UN formations involved was the US 2nd Infantry Division, which that night was forced back two miles down the Chongchon River. During the next four days the CPVA cut the division to pieces, catching it repeatedly in the flanks when in column. It lost all its guns, most of its transport and suffered nearly 80 per cent casualties. On the evening of the 26th, the entire ROK II Corps was under heavy pressure in the area of Tokchon, on the Taedong River. The Turkish Brigade was sent to Kunuri to help the ROK troops, but was repeatedly ambushed along the road, and eventually scattered. The 27th British Commonwealth Brigade was ordered forward to help, but its route was blocked by heavy concentrations of Chinese soldiers. Elsewhere along the 8th Army front there was successful

[1] Amongst other UN troops arriving in November 1950 were the 29th British Independent Brigade, a Thailand battalion and a South African air force unit.

CPVA pressure. By the 28th, badly shocked and mauled, the 8th Army was retreating southwards, with the Chinese hot on its heels. Instead of reaching the Yalu River, UN troops were being jostled backwards. Having a wide-open right flank the 8th Army regrouped as best it could and fell back by slow stages. A scorched earth policy was adopted, retreating UN personnel demolishing or destroying anything that might be of value to the enemy.

At first it was hoped to hold the line of Pyongyang, but this city had to be evacuated on 5th December and MacArthur ordered a quick withdrawal of several miles to make a clean break, so that a defensive line could be formed about the 38th Parallel. By the 13th, UN forces had arrived at the lower reaches of the frozen Imjin River, having moved back some 120 miles in ten days, during which time there had been little or no contact with the enemy. The CPVA troops had paused to re-group around Pyongyang, where they were collecting every form of transport imaginable—farm carts, wheel barrows, trucks—ready for the next jump forward. The 8th Army was momentarily saved from further assault as the CPVA had reached the limit of its forward movement, having exhausted its supplies. The 8th Army had been badly hampered in its retreat by hordes of refugees—it was estimated that about three million people from North Korea had followed in the wake of, and amongst, the UN troops.

To the east, X Corps advanced on 24th November with the object of clearing north-east Korea. Already, on the 21st, a detachment of US troops had taken Hyesanjin, on the Yalu River (the only US troops to reach it). A ROK division entered Chongjin, on the coast, the farthest point north reached by any UN troops. There was little contact with the CPVA until the 28th, when the main action took place near the Changjin Reservoir.[1] Elements of the Marine Division, the 7th Infantry Division and ROK formations were hit in the flank during the night by six CPVA divisions. Physically separated from the 8th Army and hardly able to look after itself, let alone

---

[1] Also known as the Chosin Reservoir.

assist on the western sector, MacArthur on the 30th was ordered to withdraw X Corps from north-east Korea, lest it be lost completely. It was to be used to reinforce south-east Korea against an anticipated Chinese attack. The long, dangerous withdrawal to the port of Hungnam began. The winter had now set in firmly and with no warm clothing UN troops suffered intense hardship. Many were frozen to death. The UN elements trapped around the Changjin Reservoir had to make a hazardous retreat, since they were under constant flank attack as they withdrew along the only available road.

Hungnam was made into a strong bridgehead, held by the US 3rd Infantry Division, on which all X Corps troops concentrated. The evacuation began on 12th December, and the bridgehead, under frequent assault by the CPVA and some reconstituted North Korean units, contracted as stores and personnel were evacuated. The enemy was successfully held at bay until the evacuation was completed on the 24th, by which time some 105,000 troops, 91,000 Korean refugees, 17,300 vehicles and 91,000 tons of stores had been taken off.

The CPVA forces moved into an offensive. Each man carried enough food and ammunition to last him for five to six days, and it was noticeable that the momentum of any advance slackened after that period, as formations paused while further supplies were brought up. As these supplies were mostly carried by porters, who moved at night to avoid the attention of the UN air forces, the CPVA pauses were sometimes comparatively lengthy. Opportunities were lost, not because of neglect, but because the Chinese military supply system, primitive and slow, hampered exploitation. The CPVA travelled at night and hid by day as a matter of course, again to avoid UN reconnaissance aircraft. They also fought at night whenever possible, fearing illumination and the inevitable resultant artillery fire. Their arms at this juncture were those taken from the defeated Japanese in 1945, and those captured from the Nationalists, mainly of US manufacture, in the civil war. There were hardly any Soviet weapons in the hands of the Chinese fighting men during the initial advances.

The CPVA moved, and attacked, in close formations, mis-called at first 'mass assaults'. This was partly because they moved at night and partly because their communications were primitive and sparse, the radio network only reaching down to regiments and the telephone, where practicable, only to companies. Within the company all commands were either shouted or given by signal or whistle, and for this reason the men tended to bunch together. Mortar and artillery fire was poorly aimed and not very well controlled. The basic principle of the CPVA assault operation was to move at night in over-whelming strength against the flanks and rear of UN units, first surprising and then overrunning the sub-units in a series of attacks. The assault was accompanied by loud noises, such as bugle and whistle sounds and shouts. Sometimes the assaults were preceded by mortar barrages. The tactics became mechanical, enabling UN forces at times to anticipate CPVA moves, and to inflict heavy casualties. Chinese attacks were forced home with total disregard of loss. To the CPVA it was an infantry war, fought on foot by self-sufficient soldiers, with extremely good cross-country and night-marching capabilities. The chief exception to this was initially in the west, where the Chinese used two cavalry formations, mounted on sturdy Mongolian ponies, against the 8th Army, and this gave them excellent mobility away from the roads. The cavalry contingent soon disappeared from the scene, however, as the problem of providing fodder cancelled out its tactical value.

During the first month of the Chinese invasion of Korea, a joint KPA-CPVA GHQ was established at Mukden, nominally under the leadership of Kim Il-sung, the Premier of North Korea, but actually under the command of General Lin Piao. Soon General Lin moved into Korea in the wake of his armies, but the combined GHQ was retained to preserve the fiction of Chinese 'volunteers', for political reasons and as a sop to North Korean susceptibilities. The overall direction of the war was still in Soviet hands, and was controlled by the Soviet Military Mission which formulated plans at GHQ.

On 23rd December, General Walker was killed in a road

accident, and his successor was Lieutenant-General Matthew B. Ridgway, who took command on the 24th, the day the 8th Army fell back across the 38th Parallel. Ridgway was US Deputy Chief of Staff for Army Administration, and in World War II had commanded the 82nd Airborne Division and the 18th Airborne Corps.

On the 27th, X Corps became part of the 8th Army. There had been difficulties in co-ordinating the activities of these two entirely separate formations in Korea throughout the war, and the situation was clearly unsatisfactory from every point of view, strategical, logistical and tactical. It had been due simply to MacArthur's insistence that the 8th Army and X Corps should remain independent of each other; but now, under pressure from the Joint Chiefs of Staff, the command of all UN ground forces in Korea was unified. General Ridgway was given complete authority to plan and execute operations in Korea, and MacArthur ceased to exercise close supervision over the battlefield. Ridgway took over command at a critical moment, when UN forces were being pushed backwards by the CPVA. His first task was to stabilize a defence line as quickly as he could, and then to stimulate his army into a counter-advance.

With its supply position once again a satisfactory one, the CPVA was ready to move and the advance against the 8th Army was resumed on the last day of the year. Again envelopment tactics were employed successfully against UN formations by seven Chinese armies and two North Korean corps. On 4th January (1951), the CPVA took Seoul, and the bridges over the Han River were blown by UN troops. Refugees were turned back at gun point. The Kimpo airfield had been abandoned a day previously, and huge stocks of napalm and fuel were destroyed there. On the 4th Inchon was also evacuated.

By withdrawing rapidly to prevent himself being outflanked, Ridgway was able by 24th January to stabilize a defence line that ran across the peninsula roughly north of Ansong, south of Wonju to just north of Samchok, and on it UN troops were allowed to remain in position for the simple reason that the CPVA advance had again outrun its supplies, and also perhaps used up its store of human energy. It could not, with honesty, be claimed that UN fire power on this occasion had stopped the Chinese troops. After a retreat of nearly 300 miles, the morale of the 8th Army was—not altogether surprisingly—low; but despite nearly 13,000 UN casualties and great losses of equipment, most formations were still intact. It was fortunate for the UN forces that the CPVA was able to advance only in spurts of a few days at a time. Had the CPVA possessed a modern transport system and enough vehicles to enable it to exploit UN weaknesses, the story might have been a very different one.

During the long retreat of the 8th Army, UN air forces had been heavily engaged in a close support role and this, together with interdiction tasks, resulted in heavy Chinese casualties and often eased pressure on UN troops. In addition, UN aircraft began strategic bombing of industrial targets in North Korea. An improved fighter-interceptor plane, the F-86 (Sabre Jet), first appeared in the Korean skies on 18th December (1950).

The sudden, dramatic turn of the tide of war gave a deep shock to Western opinion. Hopes of a united Korea vanished as did the hope of an early end to hostilities. Another fact that shook the West was the realization that China was now a military power whose meagrely equipped army had rudely and roughly pushed the UN forces backwards. Inevitably, as the loser, MacArthur came in for criticism, especially over the failure of his intelligence service which had failed to anticipate Chinese intentions, and to foresee the huge number of Chinese soldiers that had poured secretly into Korea. The independent Central Intelligence Agency, the CIA, had been virtually banned from Korea since the Inchon Landing, although MacArthur formally denied this. He was also criticized for his handling of the UN ground forces, for keeping X Corps as a separate formation and for refusing to establish a firm defence line on the 'waist' of the peninsula before advancing further northwards.

MacArthur, when he realized how many thousands of

Chinese troops his men were facing, wanted to carry out strategic bombing over the Yalu River of bases, factories, installations and communications, and he reversed his former opinion (on 28th November) and asked for the use of Chinese Nationalist troops in Korea. The Joint Chiefs of Staff, in Washington, would not permit this. In December, MacArthur suggested introducing Chinese Nationalist troops to the Chinese mainland, probably through Hong Kong, and a UN blockade of the Chinese coast. This too was vetoed. MacArthur became depressed, and formed the impression that the Joint Chiefs of Staff had lost the will to win in Korea. This was not the case: they gave a higher priority to Europe, and from a distance saw the dangers of escalation more clearly.

The possible use of atomic bombs was in many people's minds, and on 30th November (1950), Truman had been trapped into making a statement at a Press conference to the effect that he might use 'whatever weapons the US had'.[1] In fact, it was probable that there was never any real intention of using atomic bombs in the Far East at this juncture, although the Joint Chiefs of Staff, once they realized the strength of the enemy in Korea, are believed to have recommended it. There was considerable reaction overseas to Truman's statement, especially in the British Labour Party, and a hundred Members of Parliament signed a letter of protest to the Prime Minister. On 3rd December Mr. Attlee flew to Washington to confer with President Truman and, after this meeting, a pacific statement was issued.

The UN reverse in Korea caused anxiety for the safety of Japan, now denuded of Allied fighting units. MacArthur was trying to build up the newly established Japanese National

---

[1] The reported words were:

President Truman	' . . . We will take whatever steps are necessary to meet the military situation, just as we always have.'
Press Question	'Will that include the atomic bomb?'
Truman	'That will include any weapon we have.'
Press Question	'Does that mean there is active consideration of the use of the atomic bomb?'
Truman	'There has always been active consideration of its use. I don't want to see it used.'

Police Reserve so that there would be some protection and assistance in the event of a sudden Communist move in this direction. In December, more infantry weapons became available for issue, but there were differing opinions as to how they should be allocated. MacArthur wanted them for the Japanese National Police Reserve so that the defence of Japan, his primary responsibility, would be strengthened.

Syngman Rhee wanted them for his own troops. In fact, one of the suggestions from Washington had been that they should be used to arm an extra 100,000 men for the ROK forces, to bring their armed strength up to about 300,000. MacArthur opposed this, arguing that many US infantry-type arms had already been given to South Korean formations, of which some had been redistributed by Syngman Rhee to his youth organizations, which were political in nature, while others had found their way into the hands of anti-Rhee and anti-UN guerrillas active in the mountains behind the UN lines. It was pointed out that much valuable US equipment given to the ROK forces had already been lost without much compensatory injury being inflicted on the enemy, and that some ROK units had on occasions abandoned arms without fighting. MacArthur felt that a further improvement in military leadership and in training of officers and non-commissioned officers should be made before more arms were entrusted to the ROK forces, and before any expansion was seriously contemplated.

It was commonly believed that China had been secretly preparing for many months to step in should the North Koreans be in danger of defeat, but this cannot in fact have been the case. For example, the CPVA was armed with old weapons which it had possessed for several years, and no deliveries of modern Soviet military material reached Chinese formations in the field until the end of the year. Again, many of the reinforcements required to fill the divisions were not drafted into the CPVA until a few days before they marched towards Korea. Also, the formations themselves were in many instances kept on productive labour in Manchuria instead of seriously training for war until shortly before they were ordered to move to the

Yalu River. So far as can be discovered, even when on the
march units were not told they were going to fight in Korea
until they neared the Yalu. No special indoctrination was given
before they moved into Korea, beyond the stepping up of the
'Hate America' campaign that was sweeping China. Once
across the frontier the political aspect of the war and its aims
were more firmly emphasized, although the degree in which it
was rammed home to the Chinese infantryman seems to have
varied considerably from unit to unit. All this points to a hasty
decision rather than one that had been taken many months
beforehand—so there may perhaps be some partial excuse for
the failure of MacArthur's intelligence service.

China had taken a calculated risk by entering the war in
Korea, but it remained hesitant and cautious, waiting for
Western reaction and insisting that its regular soldiers were
merely 'volunteers'. Perhaps the very success of the CPVA
surprised the Chinese leaders, and emboldened them. The
CPVA had been weaker than the UN forces, in both manpower
and firepower, and despite that had been victorious. Certain
strengths and weaknesses of the Chinese armies had been
revealed. The highest praise is due to China for concentrating,
organizing, moving and deploying to battle positions about
300,000 men in complete secrecy. Muddle there had been in
plenty but positive achievement overshadowed it. The Chinese
soldiers were tough and disciplined but had poor weapons,
indifferent communications and little idea of co-ordinated
movement when once committed into action. The road-bound
UN forces played into their hands, offering easy ambush and
flanking targets. Even heavy losses did not deter the Chinese
soldiers from pressing forward to take an objective but battlefield confusion soon caused them to drift, and operations often
degenerated into a shambles. Mao Tse-tung's principle of
massing overwhelming numbers against a selected point usually
won the day. When halted to wait for supplies, they would have
been extremely vulnerable to well-directed counter-attack.

CHAPTER 6

Ridgway's Counter-offensive

In late January 1951 the two sides drew apart, the UN forces to recover and regroup and the CPVA to await further supplies, weapons and ammunition. After a pause, patrol probing by UN troops developed into a series of operations designed to push the UN line northward and, despite Chinese counter-moves in February, these succeeded in advancing it to beyond the 38th Parallel. This process continued until about the third week in April, when stiffer resistance was suddenly encountered. The hard, cold Korean winter settled on the country and the CPVA, whose strength rose to about 486,000 during this period, had acute supply difficulties. Lacking transport by the end of 1950, it was using about 300,000 conscripted porters to move some 500 tons of supplies required by the Communist formations each day. They plodded slowly in long files at night to avoid attention from the UN air forces, since during daylight the Chinese divisions were continually bombed, strafed and machine-gunned. The CPVA also had problems of organization, the huge numbers involved resulted in slow and cumbersome movement of formations, despite the good short-range, cross-country ability of the soldiers. Although they dug themselves in fairly well, little real shelter remained for the men as most of the buildings in towns and villages had been flattened. A substantial proportion was inadequately clad, and in consequence many—particularly those from mid-China and South China—suffered from exposure.

Like the CPVA, the UN forces also suffered from the severe weather conditions but not to the same extent, as warm clothing and other amenities began to arrive in quantity. Owing to poor roads and rugged terrain, the main problem was speedy distribution, since for most of the time everything had to be manhandled, sometimes over long distances and up hills. A Korean Service Corps was formed for labour duties and was employed mainly in carrying rations and supplies to forward positions, and in keeping the roads in as good a condition as

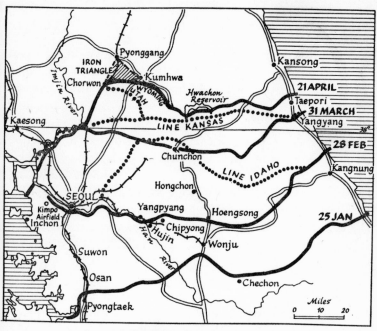

7. SUCCESSIVE UN LINES

possible. In this way UN forces, that had risen in number to over 365,000, were fed and supplied. UN forces, which moved into buildings and houses for shelter whenever possible, took an active interest in the population with which they came into contact. They helped when they could, especially in the case of children, and many orphans were adopted by military units. The integration of ROK soldiers into US divisions continued. This brought about a great reform in the American Army, in which negroes still served in all-negro units. At times in Korea, all—Americans and Koreans, negroes and whites—had fought side by side. ROK soldiers served in US units and this proved to be of value both to the US formations—still very short of manpower especially at the combat squad level—and to the ROK forces, since personnel were trained for absorption into the South Korean Army when it eventually came to be expanded.

An attempt to restore morale in the 8th Army by giving political talks on UN aims in Korea had not produced any noticeable effect. General Ridgway adopted a different approach. Disciplined, well trained men, he thought, who took a professional pride in their toughness and ability to fight, needed little in the way of ideological inspiration; and he breathed new fire and life into his command. Rumours about the 8th Army's morale had been so disturbing that at one stage there were thoughts of evacuating it from Korea to ensure its survival, and in mid-January, General J. L. Collins, the US Army Chief of Staff, visited it to assess morale and fighting ability. He reported that they were sound and improving daily under Ridgway's leadership—which by then was true. The morale crisis in the UN forces had passed.

To compare the opposing forces briefly, the CPVA lacked transport and had to make do with porters, but its proportion of 'teeth-to-tail' was high. On the other hand, despite its size, the UN forces lacked enough fighting divisions and had a much less satisfactory proportion of 'teeth-to-tail'. Control of the air enabled UN supply and administrative services to function completely and adequately, and lack of it hampered the CPVA. Morale was doubtful in some elements of the CPVA since the victorious advance had been costly in casualties and because of continual heavy aerial and other bombardment, but it was in general kept at a high level by indoctrination and by the vigilant political officers.

Towards the end of January there was a lull over the forward areas and a gap, of varying width, appeared between the two opposing forces since the CPVA withdrew slightly from places where it held indifferent tactical positions. UN patrols probed cautiously, reporting back that much of the terrain in front of UN forces was unoccupied by the enemy, so Ridgway decided to mount, on the 25th, a reconnaissance in force. It was designed primarily to seek out the positions of Chinese units and each US corps in the Western sector was authorized to use up to one US division and one ROK regiment. Known as Operation Thunderbolt, this developed into an advance that was really the beginning of the UN counter-offensive. Moving forward against scattered resistance—although a hard pocket of defence was encountered near Osan—UN units soon occupied Suwon. It was Ridgway's intention to exploit as far as he could along the west coast, but he insisted that the 8th Army maintain an unbroken line across the peninsula. To advance only along the roads, tempting though it was, would have left his flanks vulnerable to the by now well-known CPVA offensive and encroaching tactics. Making the maximum use of tanks and fire-power, UN troops combed the countryside as they moved northwards. Considerable use was made of artillery, napalm bombs and naval gun support from ships sailing just off-shore. Chinese units tended to keep away from the coastal areas that were vulnerable to naval gun-fire and the former effectiveness of the UN naval support along the west coast was somewhat reduced. The air forces gave close support by softening up enemy defensive positions and dealing with Chinese soldiers when flushed into the open. During this period the CPVA launched a few small night attacks, but generally confined itself to outpost actions, falling back in the face of superior fire power. UN tactics were to tempt the Communist soldiers back into pockets by night, surround them by day and pound them into submission.

During the last two days of January (1951) and the first few of February, CPVA resistance stiffened. Roads were mined, and artillery and mortar fire fell on UN forces in increasing density, and on some days they only were able to advance a few hundred yards. Then abruptly, on 9th February, the Chinese units withdrew a considerable distance and the UN forces were able to move forward to the Han River without encountering any organized enemy formations. A successful subsidiary action, known as Operation Punch, began on 5th February, when a task force from the US 25th Infantry Division, using co-ordinated armour, artillery and air support, fought a series of engagements for a rugged complex, known as Hill 440. When it ended, on the 9th, over 4,200 Chinese dead were counted on the battlefield. The US I Corps moved northwards and by 10th February had secured Inchon and the Kimpo airfield without firing a shot. That night UN troops in this sector closed up to the Han River.

The success of Operation Thunderbolt meant that with its left flank firmly set on the Han River, the 8th Army could make limited offensives on the central front to straighten the UN line across the peninsula, and also make enveloping threats on Seoul. Already, by 22nd January, UN patrols had reached Wonju, and X Corps units followed in their wake, encountering only light opposition. Hoengsong was occupied on 2nd February. With the object of pushing forward the UN line in the central sector and of disrupting re-grouping Communist troops to the north of Hoengsong, a limited offensive known as Operation Round Up, in which both X Corps and the ROK III Corps were involved, began on 5th February. ROK divisions from X Corps moved towards Hongchon, but ran into gradually hardening opposition on the second and third days. The ROK divisions on the right flank could not keep pace and so X Corps began to present an exposed flank. Opposition increased and, since strong enemy forces were hitting its vulnerable front, X Corps units took up blocking positions to enable ROK III Corps formations on the right to advance to envelop Hongchon. The Communists moved forces from the Western sector and, using two CPVA armies and a North Korean corps, on the night of 11th/12th launched a strong counter-attack. Its weight fell on three ROK divisions that were just to the north of Hoengsong. The Communists broke through and got to the rear of the UN forward troops in strength, where they set up road blocks and ambushes. A confused situation arose, with broken and disorganized UN units fighting desperately to break through the Communist traps to make their way southwards. Hoengsong was abandoned on the 13th, and UN troops streamed back towards Wonju.

On the night of the 13th the main CPVA assaults fell on to the positions around the cross-roads at Chipyong, to the north-west of Wonju, on the boundary of IX and X Corps. They were held by a regiment of the US 2nd Infantry Division and the French Battalion, which were soon surrounded by three CPVA divisions. Ridgway ordered these units to dig in and hold fast, and he used air drops to provide them with ammunition and supplies. The battle for the Chipyong cross-roads raged for three days during which, for the first time during the war, the CPVA really assaulted 'in mass'. But, blasted by aerial bombardment and artillery fire, the Chinese formations suffered so heavily, especially from napalm, that they were unable to overrun the UN positions. Farther to the east, once again mounting 'mass' assaults, the CPVA advanced to within a few miles of Chechon where, again, it was held by UN fire power. Then, in accordance with the usual pattern so far, the Chinese momentum slowed down after five or six days when ammunition and food ran short. The defence of Chipyong and Chechon demonstrated that CPVA 'mass' attacks—only now used for the first time—could be held by superior fire power. The UN line was quickly stabilized.

In this first phase, Ridgway seemed to have no definite major strategic aim, beyond that of pushing the enemy back, ridge by ridge, over the 38th Parallel by sheer fire power and superior force, killing as many as possible in the process. There was far more emphasis on tactics than on strategy, and the tactics were based on co-ordination of all arms, the maintenance intact of major units and of dealing out maximum punishment to the enemy.

Usually, heavy fire was put down on enemy-held hills from dawn throughout the morning, and when the objective had been saturated ground forces moved in to the assault in the afternoon. Once the enemy was displaced armour, held ready for this moment, with air support, quickly drove into the flanks of the retreating CPVA units, to inflict maximum casualties before the UN formation moved on to tackle the next feature in a similar manner. General Ridgway described this as 'Good footwork with fire power', and the tactics so evolved eventually became known as the 'Meat Grinder'. No grand scale battle took place, but the divisions, lurching forward one by one, gradually brought the UN front in line with the Han River in the Western sector.

While this was in progress a large guerrilla problem that had cropped up in the south behind the UN line was being dealt with by ROK security forces, aided by the Marine Division. During the CPVA January offensive, remnants of the North Korean II Corps, amounting to some 22,000 men, had infiltrated through the eastern mountains almost to within 20 miles of Taegu—in itself a considerable feat—where they joined up with other Communist guerrillas already in the hills there. Lying low during daylight, at night the soldiers and guerrillas would descend to the valleys to raid villages, pillage and ambush UN vehicles on roads. Marine and ROK soldiers moved out against these Communist fighters who at first showed considerable resistance when tackled. Groups were surrounded in the regions of Andong and Uisong, and then pounded with mortar fire. These tactics reduced the general aggressiveness, and before long the guerrillas usually disappeared after an initial exchange of shots. By mid-February, the number of regular active North Korean guerrillas behind the UN line in this region had been reduced to about 18,000,[1] and the Marine Division could be released to assist on the main front.

On the 18th (February) reports from his forward units pointed to a CPVA withdrawal, so General Ridgway immediately ordered X Corps to attack eastwards near Chechon, to destroy the North Korean soldiers on the east flank. At the same time, IX Corps was to seize positions along the line from

[1] Numbers of Communist guerrillas behind the UN line have never been assessed with any certainty, and such figures must be treated with reserve—but they are the only ones available.

Hujin to Yangpyong. By the end of the day initiative all along the front had passed to the UN forces.

Empty fox-holes and abandoned weapons and equipment indicated a hasty retreat by the CPVA in the central sector, but at first this was thought to be a ruse, and UN Forces advanced warily. But, weakened by ground and air action, hungry and inadequately clad, the CPVA had outrun its supply services, and was suffering badly from typhus, frost-bite and trench foot. Morale had been sapped by heavy casualties. Taking instant advantage of this favourable situation Ridgway initiated Operation Killer, which began on 21st February. This was a limited central front offensive, aimed at pushing the UN line level with the lower reaches of the Han River, denying certain tactical positions to the enemy, and securing part of the lateral road from Wonju to Kangnung. With the operation the emphasis changed from one of primarily taking ground to one of primarily destroying the enemy. Both the I and X Corps were involved, and the Marine Division, recently engaged in anti-guerrilla operations, was brought into X Corps and committed near Wonju. In all, seven UN divisions moved forward intent upon destroying as many CPVA formations as possible. Across a 60-mile front swollen streams and mud hampered operations and slowed the advance, while the mountainous terrain and continual rain provided severe tests of endurance for the UN soldiers. Groups of Chinese troops contested the advance, but clearly they had a delaying mission only and by the 24th the Marines were overlooking Hoengsong.

The CPVA had been more badly mauled than was realized, and many of the positions overrun were littered with enemy dead. More bodies were found as UN divisions moved forward, and many others were discovered in hastily dug, shallow graves. The Psychological Warfare Branch came into action, and the US 5th Air Force dropped thousands of leaflets, many saying 'Count your Men'—one of the most devastating psychological phrases of the war, which had its effect on the retreating Chinese troops.

By the 28th, all active pockets of the CPVA south of the Han

River had collapsed, and next day the UN line across the peninsula was made firm. As the thaw set in, the river became an obstacle, momentarily checking further progress. But for the time being the entire 8th Army front was stable and intact, with no gaps or dangerous salients poking into it. This had been largely accomplished by well co-ordinated fire power and movement, but nevertheless the bulk of the enemy had managed to withdraw, while adverse weather disrupted UN communications and movement.

Another push northwards, known as Operation Ripper, was planned on the central front with the IX and X Corps detailed to seize Hongchon, Chunchon, and positions along a line named Idaho, just south of the 38th Parallel. It was designed to outflank Seoul and also to try to divorce the CPVA from the North Korean formations in the east. I Corps, just south of Seoul, was to remain temporarily in position, while ROK units were to protect the right flanks. The accent was on destroying as many Chinese personnel as possible. Operation Ripper commenced on 7th March when, after the heaviest artillery bombardment so far in the war, the US 25th Infantry Division forced its way across the Han River. For three days the CPVA resisted strongly; then it gave way and retired in disorder, the Communists suffering heavily. It is believed that in 24 hours (7th/8th March) they had over 21,000 casualties. Elsewhere along the front UN troops made steady but unspectacular gains against small unit delaying actions. A slow, grinding type of warfare developed. By the 13th, all formations had completed the first part of the operation, and the advance towards Line Idaho commenced the next day. Troops from I Corps, on the west, crossed the Han River, and were able to move to the outskirts of Seoul before running into desultory enemy fire. The city was found to be almost deserted, and on the night of 14th/15th UN troops moved in and took possession. Seoul had already been hard hit by battle; there were many destroyed and damaged buildings, no municipal services were operating, and only about 200,000 civilians remained.

To the east the ROK I Corps was ordered to destroy the

remnants of the North Korean division in the Chungbong Mountains, south-west of the coastal town of Kangnung, which had infiltrated through in January. During the third week in March, ROK units moved against the North Koreans, but although many casualties were inflicted, the majority of the enemy escaped northwards. In this sector UN forces reached Line Idaho by the 17th. In the centre, the IX and X Corps slogged forward, encountering delaying enemy in deep bunkers. Hongchon was secured, and so was Chunchon, but at times resistance was hard, as each enemy pocket was on a peak that had to be enveloped and dealt with separately. The thaw turned the ground in the valleys into a morass, which retarded movement. In the west, when Seoul had fallen, I Corps was ordered to move towards the Imjin River, beginning its advance on the 22nd. On the 23rd, paratroops were dropped ahead of the advancing forces in an attempt to trap the CPVA by blocking the road from Seoul to Kaesong, but the Communists fell back quickly and few prisoners were taken. The move to the Imjin River in this sector was fairly speedy. As UN units reached Line Idaho in the last days of March, Operation Ripper slowed down. Although terrain had been taken, the main body of the CPVA had rolled with the punch, and escaped destruction by withdrawing to a prepared defensive line just to the north of the 38th Parallel, the strongest part of which became known as the Iron Triangle. This lay between Chorwon, Kumhwa and Pyonggang,[1] where a series of fortifications and shelters had been built in the rock, reinforced by concrete and logs.

Once Line Idaho had been reached, the problem had to be faced of whether or not to recross the 38th Parallel. The decision was passed by President Truman to General Ridgway, since at this juncture it was regarded as strategical rather than political. MacArthur reckoned that he could advance with advantage up to 100 miles north of the 38th Parallel, after which UN air superiority would be nullified to a large extent by the lengthening UN supply lines and the correspondingly

[1] Not to be confused with Pyongyang, the Capital of North Korea.

much shorter ones of the CPVA. Ridgway realized that the CPVA was re-grouping and reorganizing for a counter-attack, and that March to July was the rainy season when the terrain would become extremely difficult for vehicles. With MacArthur's approval, he chose to continue to advance.

Accordingly, Operation Rugged succeeded Operation Ripper on 5th April, with the object of pushing forward to a new line across the peninsula—Line Kansas—which ran along good tactical ground just north of the 38th Parallel. By the 9th, UN forces were on this new line, which included in the centre the Hwachon Reservoir, Seoul's source of water and electric power. The enemy opened the sluice gates of the reservoir, causing the Pukhan River to rise, making it difficult to bridge. Raids launched to prevent the Chinese troops from opening other sluice gates failed, mainly because of poor visibility and lack of landing-craft. By the 10th, there were six UN divisions north of the 38th Parallel. Next, I Corps and units of IX Corps moved forward towards Chorwon, the south-west corner of the Iron Triangle, with the intention of moving to a line, Line Utah, which was an outward bulge of Line Kansas.

Generally, during April, UN units edged forward all along the front. It seemed as though the CPVA was still in retreat, although small units were left to fight delaying actions. Chinese troops still usually attacked at night when UN forces could not use air support to hit back decisively. The first signs of an attack were flares and mortar fire; next came a thin line of sub-machine-gunners and grenade-throwers; then snipers worked their way well forward. These small assaults lasted until one side or the other—usually, but not always, the Communists—ran out of ammunition; and in any event CPVA assaults usually died away at dawn. UN tactics were based on daylight attacks on narrow fronts on delaying strong points, with ample artillery and air support. Sometimes the Chinese forces burned large areas to make smoke screens to reduce the accuracy of air support. At night, UN troops usually drew themselves into defensive perimeters. In many places UN troops were completely out of contact with the CPVA.

By 19th April, Ridgway's divisions were in position along Line Utah. After a brief pause another advance was ordered to a new line, Line Wyoming, which was a bulge extension of Line Utah to the east. If this move proved successful it would mean that UN forces would be able to look down on Chorwon. But suddenly, on the 22nd, enemy activity became noticeable along the whole front, and resistance hardened considerably.

Throughout this phase warships from several UN countries, including Britain, the Netherlands and New Zealand, maintained an effective blockade and harassed the coasts of North Korea. They continually, for example, bombarded Wonsan and Songjin, two communication centres on the east coast. Also, several commando raids were carried out to capture prisoners, gain information and damage morale. ROK units raided Iwon, Inchon, and other places. The UN air forces, too, were extremely active. Light bombers of the US Air Force, and heavier aircraft of the US Far East Air Force ranged over North Korea, concentrating upon supply points, communication centres and interdiction targets.

Until now, the UN air forces completely dominated the skies, but evidence began to come in of increasing Chinese air strength and it was observed that many airfields were being constructed in North Korea. By mid-April it was estimated that the CPVA had about 750 planes of Soviet origin, all safely based north of the Yalu River. They did not venture far over the frontier, and were seldom seen near a battlefield; at the first sign of UN aircraft in the skies they scurried home again. The first show of Communist air strength and the first major clash between the two air forces occurred on 12th April, when 48 B-29s (Superfortresses) escorted by 75 fighters, were on a mission to bomb bridges over the Yalu River at Antung and Sinuiju. They were attacked by about 80 MiG-15s, and in the ensuing fight, although 9 MiGs were brought down, three UN planes were lost and seven others damaged. The Chinese air force, non-existent a few weeks before, had become a serious factor in the war.

A brief summary of this phase which lasted about three

months. In late January, after the CPVA offensive, the UN line had been stabilized, and in February, a Chinese offensive in the central sector had been held. Then by a series of operations the UN line was pushed northwards, against delaying opposition, across the 38th Parallel. Further advances were made until 21st April, by which time UN forces held a line across the peninsula from Taepori, on the east coast, through the Hwachon Reservoir, touching the Iron Triangle, and south-west to Munsan.[1] During this period, with the exception of the February offensive, the CPVA had been engaged on defensive withdrawal, but the slow UN follow-up movement had allowed the bulk of the Chinese soldiers to retreat to safety, and few pincer movements had succeeded in their objective of trapping large bodies of the enemy.

[1] Sometimes shown on maps as Munsan-ni.

CHAPTER 7

The MacArthur Plan

Meanwhile, a combination of events led to the abrupt dismissal of General MacArthur, the CICUNC, who had devised a plan for ending the war quickly and decisively. The Korean War was becoming unpopular in America, where all objected to the high taxation it necessitated and younger men in particular to being drafted to fight again so soon after World War II. There was dissatisfaction over the way in which it was conducted, and alarm at the unexpected appearance of so many Chinese troops. At the same time there was a mounting fear of Soviet threats, which caused America to reinforce its troops in Germany. Many felt that the first overall priority should be to keep the UN and that NATO front intact, and to do everything possible to strengthen Western strength in Europe. They felt that the war in Korea was a deliberate diversion, designed to detract attention from the main enemy—the Soviet Union. This was the view of President Truman and the Joint Chiefs of Staff. As the General in charge of operations, MacArthur was naturally anxious to use all possible means to bring the war to a victorious conclusion, and he saw some of these deliberately withheld. He saw, for example, Chiang Kai-shek's army cooped up on Formosa, when it could have been moved either to swell the UN force in Korea or to be let loose on the Chinese mainland. Rather than risk defeat, or a prolonged struggle, he would have liked to use atomic weapons to cripple the enemy; and he would have liked, too, to carry the war into Manchuria to shatter the inviolable sanctuary of the Chinese forces.

In mid-February 1951, when the UN line was briefly

stabilized just south of Seoul, MacArthur formulated a plan that was bold but extremely controversial. Not every detail of it has been published, but sufficient information has been revealed by MacArthur, and others, to enable us to speculate with a fair degree of certainty about its broad outlines. At this time there were just under half a million UN troops in Korea, facing, MacArthur estimated, about 1 million Chinese and a few thousand North Koreans. In fact it is more probable there were only about 850,000 Communist soldiers in Korea at this moment, the difference in the estimate being due to UN intelligence faults. There were another 4 million soldiers in the Chinese Army back in China itself.

The main features of the plan were—

1. To use 20 to 30 atomic bombs to destroy Chinese air installations and supply bases in Manchuria.
2. To lay a radio-active belt of nuclear material across the northern neck of the peninsula.
3. To use the 500,000 Nationalist Chinese troops from Formosa (plus two Marine divisions) to make amphibious and air landings simultaneously on both the east and the west coasts of the neck of Korea, to join up overland and so cut off and contain the CPVA.
4. To move a reinforced 8th Army northwards to crush the trapped CPVA.

MacArthur estimated that within ten days from the moment he put this plan into operation he would have forced the CPVA in Korea to capitulate completely and would have brought the war to an end with a minimum loss of life on the UN side.

This plan was rejected by President Truman and the Joint Chiefs of Staff in Washington and condemned by those Western statesmen who came to know of it. The reaction of Mr. Attlee, the British Prime Minister, when he suspected that the use of atomic bombs was under consideration, has been mentioned. In America, Democrat leaders were against the plan, but some prominent Republicans were in favour of it—or at any rate part of it.

Although it was rejected, it may be of interest to discuss it briefly, and to consider in retrospect whether it would have been successful. Would it have sparked off World War III as so many feared? The controversial features were the proposed use of atomic bombs, the extension of the war into China and the use of Chinese Nationalist troops. The use of atomic bombs might bring the Soviet Union into the conflict; the bombing of Manchuria might bring China openly into the war in Korea against UN forces; and the use of Chinese Nationalist troops might reopen the Chinese civil war.

The Soviet Union, at that time, was in a very inferior nuclear position. The USA had exploded its first atomic device in June 1945, and in the intervening years had built up a stockpile. Just how many atomic bombs were in that US stockpile in 1951 has not been revealed, but as General MacArthur was prepared to expend up to 30 of them in Korea, it was probably several times that number. The Soviet Union, on the other hand, which had exploded its first atomic device in August 1949, barely 18 months previously, could only have had a tiny stockpile[1] available, and it seems unlikely that the Soviet Union would have risked a nuclear conflict that would have been so one-sided. Moreover, America not only had atomic bombs in quantity, but had the means to deliver them in the shape of a fleet of long-range bombers; indeed, it was well known at this period that the essence of American defence strategy was that of total nuclear retaliation. The Soviet Union, having concentrated upon close-support aircraft during World War II, had no such fleet of strategic bombers, but was in the process of building one, and so probably would have been unable to deliver effectively the few atomic bombs it had. Although fear of escalation into World War III, on the atomic bomb factor alone, loomed large in Western eyes in 1951, in retrospect the

[1] Hydrogen bombs had not yet appeared on the scene. The USA was due to explode its first hydrogen bomb in November 1952. The expression 'nuclear' embraces both atomic and hydrogen weapons.

It is of interest to note that on 1st September 1950, the Commandant of the US Air War College was suspended for saying that he could break up the 'five Russian A-nests within a week'.

risk does not seem nearly as great as it then appeared to be. Apart from purely military considerations, on the political side, too, there is considerable doubt about whether the Soviet Union would have intervened to help China had that country been attacked. Stalin may well have wanted a weak, divided China at his back door, while he faced the hostile West.

Many thought that to bomb targets in Manchuria would cause China to enter the war openly and throw its five million soldiers against the puny UN force; but, on reconsideration, these fears seem to have been exaggerated. It was true that US prestige had taken a heavy tumble in Asia, partly by having supported the losing side in the civil war and partly by having been hastily jostled backwards in Korea in November and December (1950) by the CPVA. Militarily and economically desperately weak, however, China was so uncertain and bewildered by its own internal situation that one can only marvel at Mao Tse-tung's decision to commit up to one million of his best soldiers in Korea. There may well have been skilful persuasion by Stalin. Less than 18 months had passed since the Chinese People's Republic had been established, and although the Communists were in possession of most of the mainland, they were not yet its complete masters and still had considerable opposition, both material and ideological. The inherent weaknesses of the Chinese Army which failed in its assault on Quemoy in October 1949, did not occupy Hainan Island until April 1950, and had not yet attempted to subdue Formosa have been mentioned. The invasion of Tibet, begun in October 1950, was running into difficulties.

China had secretly and with apparent reluctance entered the war in Korea, crossing the Yalu River like a thief in the night. For some time this invasion was kept secret, and it was only weeks later, when its huge size could no longer be concealed, that the Chinese Government admitted there were 'Chinese volunteers' fighting in Korea. In this initial stage there was much apprehension of retaliation, as was evidenced by the mushroom-like appearance of air raid shelters in the cities and towns of Manchuria, and the frequent air raid drills practised by the population. The Chinese Army was ill-armed and poorly equipped—a shambling mass of infantry. The best part of it was in Korea, slowly being armed with modern Soviet small arms and guns—obviously part of the bargain between Stalin and Mao Tse-tung. The overall picture is not of a war-mad China anxious to leap into any fray, but rather of an unwilling aggressor, prodded from behind.

It would have been of little advantage to China to have entered the war openly in Korea. Its bases and cities would then have been subjected to aerial attacks by UN air forces, and the sanctuary north of the Yalu River, so valuable if not essential to the CPVA, would no longer have been safe. Also, its entry into the war would almost certainly have provoked the USA into reversing its policy of restraining Chiang Kai-shek. An interesting sidelight on this has since been revealed, in the MacArthur *Reminiscences*, when he tells of an official leaflet published in China by General Lin Piao, the commander of the CPVA, which indicated that the Chinese general would not have 'risked his reputation and his men' (an interesting order of risks) if he had not been assured that the Americans would not take measures against his supply lines. This seems to mean that Chinese troops would not have been committed against UN forces until it was certain that the US would not carry the war into China, or indeed allow Chiang Kai-shek to do so either. MacArthur was convinced there was a security leak from Washington[1] to Peking, which gave the Chinese leaders much information about the discussions and decisions of Western statesmen. There may have been something in this, for the Chinese seemed to know, with uncanny accuracy, exactly how far to go without provoking UN retaliation on Chinese territory.

It is frequently said that the US 7th Fleet, patrolling the

[1] In 1956, General MacArthur alleged that Guy Burgess and Donald MacLean, British spies who had defected to the Soviet Union in 1951, had been implicated in passing on information about his plans to the Communists. He was of the opinion that every message he sent to Washington was shown to the British by the State Department, and that this information was then relayed either through India, or the Soviet Embassy in London, to Peking.

Straits of Formosa, was there not so much to prevent the Chinese invading the island as to restrain Chiang Kai-shek from launching an invasion. Having recovered to some extent from his defeats, with his army now largely re-equipped with US material and better trained than it had ever been before, Chiang Kai-shek was eager to get into action against the Communists. He did not mind whether it was in Korea or on the mainland. He felt that this was the right moment; the Communist Chinese Army was full of Nationalist turncoats, not yet brain-washed into Communism, and in China there were many active centres of resistance and guerrilla pockets. The Americans feared that if the Chinese civil war reopened they would be committed to supporting the Nationalists openly, and that vast quantities of arms, money and men would be sucked into the resulting imbroglio at a time when the chief threat to world peace was not in Asia but in Europe. There was no doubt, from Chiang Kai-shek's point of view, that this was an opportune moment to reopen hostilities; and, had he done so, his chances of success would not have been so hopeless as many suggest. Had this been allowed to happen, there might today be two 'Chinas', each antagonistic to the other and perhaps locked together in almost perpetual guerrilla warfare. The Chinese would not be the danger to the world today that in fact they are.

Assuming that political objections could have been overcome and risks accepted, what would have been the chances of success of the MacArthur Plan? Just how feasible was it? The atomic bombing of the Manchurian military centres would have disrupted supplies, but would not have stopped them completely. MacArthur appreciated this fact, and the radioactive belt he wanted to lay across the northern part of the Korean peninsula was designed to complement the atomic strikes and effectively to complete the sealing off of the CPVA in Korea. The radiation belt, five miles wide, was to consist of cobalt and was to be laid by both aircraft and vehicles. He thought cobalt had a 'half-life' of sixty years, and although five years might have been more accurate, this was irrelevant to the plan, which aimed at bringing the war to an end in ten days. In fact, the cobalt could only have been dropped from aircraft in flakes, and could not, as MacArthur supposed, be sown from vehicles. This meant that instead of taking hours to lay the radiation belt, it would have taken days. But it was a practical proposition and, once laid, it would have served its purpose, which was to provide a barrier that would block supplies being brought into Korea by land, and prevent mass break-outs from the south. It was assumed, of course, that sufficient cobalt was available.

By this time Korea was a devastated waste, and as all CPVA ammunition and food had to be brought in from Manchuria, MacArthur's starvation operation would probably have succeeded. As has been seen, the CPVA usually seemed to stock up with supplies and ammunition for a five to seven-day period only, after which they had to be replenished. It was on this analysis that General MacArthur obviously estimated that within ten days the Communist soldiers would be starving and impotent, having used up all their food and ammunition. As the CPVA had no supply depots of any size inside Korea, most being across the Yalu River, he was most probably correct. Also, mass break-outs of groups of desperately hungry soldiers would have been foiled by the radiation belt, and any who got through would have died within days of setting foot in Manchuria.

In addition to the starvation weapon, it was his intention to land some half-million soldiers, mainly Nationalist Chinese, on either side of the neck of the peninsula. To move that number of men in ships and aircraft would have been a considerable operation, but presumably MacArthur's staff had worked this out in detail and were satisfied that transport was available, or could quickly be made available. It should be remarked that MacArthur had considerable experience of moving large bodies of troops long distances in the Pacific theatre in World War II, and his Inchon Landing showed that he had not lost his flair. Assuming that half a million troops could be transported, they would have been able to close the pincer by moving towards each other across country to trap and cut off the CPVA. With ample ammunition and air support, and fighting against an enemy with rapidly dwindling supplies, they should certainly have been able to accomplish this. Chinese would have been fighting Chinese and many doubted Nationalist fighting capability after the débâcle on the mainland. They were reportedly ill-organized, unreliable and demoralized, but MacArthur had recently inspected them on Formosa and must have been sufficiently impressed by what he saw to include them in his plan. The last phase of the plan was the crushing movement, the striking of the hammer against the anvil formed by the Nationalist Chinese in the north, the final annihilation, when reinforced UN forces would have moved relentlessly forward almost in line across the country. This too could have been achieved. The superior fire power of the UN divisions would have prevailed against that of the less-well-armed CPVA, which would, of course, have been handicapped by an increasing ammunition supply problem. In addition, the CPVA had an acute health problem. It was plagued with typhus and other diseases and suffered from a shortage of drugs and medicines. Cutting off all supplies and blocking evacuation completely would have aggravated this immensely.

The conclusion probably is that if General MacArthur had been allowed to carry out his plan—and if it could have been put into operation fairly speedily—it would have been successful. Almost one million Chinese soldiers and the remnants of the North Korean forces would have been trapped and either annihilated or taken prisoner within a fortnight, and the war brought to a successful conclusion. It is on balance improbable that this would have either ignited World War III, or reopened the Chinese civil war. However, it was not to be and the war was to drag on. As so often, cautious counsels prevailed, and fear of the Soviet Union was a potent factor.

MacArthur was naturally very disappointed at the rejection of his plan and felt that he was being deliberately deprived of the tools needed to finish the job. He did not agree with General Omar Bradley, the Chairman of the US Joint Chiefs of Staff, who said it was 'the wrong war, at the wrong place at the wrong time with the wrong enemy', and he spoke out openly against the stalemate. He had always wanted to push across the Yalu River and hit the CPVA bases in Manchuria, and although overtly accepting the decision of the Joint Chiefs of Staff, he made several statements that contrasted with official policy. MacArthur considered this decision to be one more move against him in his deepening feud with the Joint Chiefs of Staff.

The Wake Island meeting of October (1950) had not been a success; and as MacArthur's prediction that the Chinese would not enter the war had been wrong, the US Administration was not impressed by his arguments. He was also the subject of British reprobation. Attlee, the Prime Minister, had little taste for a flamboyant, proconsul-type general and criticized his handling of the war and in particular the shortcomings of the intelligence services in Korea. Friction between General MacArthur and the US Administration came to a head in March, when he released his 'military appraisal', which included an offer to meet the enemy Commander-in-Chief in the field to negotiate. It occurred at a time when there were hopes of a truce and of peace talks. It was completely unauthorized and forestalled a statement President Truman was about to issue saying that the fighting must continue until a settlement was reached. MacArthur believed that the fighting should go on and be forced to a successful conclusion rather than be resolved politically, which was a challenge to the Governments both at Peking and Washington. Peking rejected the offer to negotiate.

In Washington another matter was coming to a climax, MacArthur's correspondence with Senator Joseph W. Martin, who had written to him asking for comments on a suggestion that Chiang Kai-shek's forces should be allowed to land on the mainland. MacArthur replied in favour of this suggestion, the letter being dated 20th March. This letter of MacArthur's, which advocated the 'meeting of force with the maximum counter-force', and ending with 'There is no substitute for Victory', was read out on the floor of the Senate on 5th April.

Owing to MacArthur's previous scarcely-veiled disapproval of the way in which his Government was conducting the war, in December (1950) Truman had ordered that all public statements by theatre commanders should be first cleared through Washington, an instruction frequently ignored by MacArthur. Apparently twice before Truman had thought seriously of dismissing General MacArthur, but had not done so.

According to his 'Memoirs', the President had already decided to remove MacArthur for his statement of 24th March, before the letter to Senator Martin was read out; but it was not until 11th April that MacArthur was formally relieved of his appointments and responsibilities because 'he was unable to give his whole-hearted support to the Administration and the UN'. General Ridgway was appointed in his stead. Truman had to use all his political acumen and sense of timing to prevent the Republicans mustering enough support for MacArthur, who had great military prestige in America, to prevent his dismissal. General Ridgway's successor in Korea was Lieutenant-General James Van Fleet, who had gained a sound military reputation in Greece during the Greek civil war.

Although the official reason given was that MacArthur no longer held the confidence of the Administration, the real one was that the democratic principle of civilian control over the military, even in time of war, was in dispute. MacArthur's dismissal was regarded with approval by all the Western democracies since it emphasized that the military must always be subordinate to civilian authority. Clearly the decision was absolutely correct; but it is only fair to remember in Mac-Arthur's favour that he had had to plan and fight in a hampering context of civilian hesitancy and indecision.

CHAPTER 8

Communist Offensives

Meanwhile Communist troops had been preparing to hit back, and in the next phase of this war, which lasted for about six weeks, they launched two massive offensives both of which gained ground. The first, which started on 22nd April and continued until about the 30th, drove UN forces back across the width of the peninsula to a depth of up to 35 miles or more, before it was held. Then, after a pause during which UN units crept back northwards for short distances, the second Communist offensive got under way on 15th May and lasted until about the 20th. This pushed the UN line southwards once more. But on the 18th, even before the Communist momentum had been halted, UN troops started to counter-attack. They struck northwards to re-cross the 38th Parallel and briefly to enter Pyongyang, the North Korean capital.

On 14th April, Lieutenant-General James A. Van Fleet took over command of the 8th Army, which consisted of all the UN ground forces fighting in Korea. He barely had time to settle in and make his presence felt before the first Communist offensive hit the UN line with a shattering blow. UN forces in Korea now numbered about 420,000, of which about 230,000 were in the forward areas. Basically, Van Fleet's fighting formations consisted of seven US divisions, nine ROK divisions (the tenth was not activated fully until June), two British and one Turkish brigade. Other national contingents were of battalion size, or even less, and were placed either within existing US or British formations, or attached to them. US divisions were now up to strength, each averaging about 18,000 all ranks, but to achieve this a sizeable number of KATUSA personnel were included in them. The divisions were well armed and equipped, and had considerable fire potential. For example, each had four artillery units and an armoured element. The US divisions and the British and Turkish brigades were distributed into three corps, which were (from west to east) the I, the IX and the X, extending from the Yellow Sea to about three-quarters of the way across the peninsula. The eastern sector was held by ROK troops, organized into two corps, the ROK I and the ROK III. These contained the majority of the ROK divisions, and the remainder were sandwiched between US divisions to the west or in reserve. ROK divisions were weaker numerically, had no organic artillery or armour and very little modern transport. Supporting General Van Fleet were the powerful US Far East Air Force, the US 5th Air Force and Marine and naval aircraft. Also, naval support was given by ships of several UN countries, which harassed the Communist coastline, and in the east provided close artillery fire for ROK formations.

The combined KPA-CPVA GHQ was in the hills near Pyongyang, the nominal commander still being Kim Il-sung, who most probably by now had only a very minor say in the conduct of the war. Major decisions on war strategy were taken either by the Russians or the Chinese, with the Russians usually having the final word. A large staff of Soviet military officers was maintained at the joint GHQ, headed by Colonel-General Shykov, the Soviet Ambassador to North Korea; and, as the Soviet Union supplied the modern arms, aircraft, vehicles, fuel and most of the ammunition that made it possible for the Chinese and North Korean Communists to fight against the UN forces, it is almost certain that Stalin insisted upon guiding strategy. But it was done tactfully. Although directives were drafted in Russian, itself an indication of where the power lay, a façade of North Korean independence was maintained. Soviet officers remained in the background and were never seen giving orders.

On the other hand, the bulk of the fighting manpower came

from China, in the shape of the CPVA. Without it the war in Korea could not have been continued for another day, and so it might have been expected that Mao Tse-tung would have demanded a say in how the war was conducted. In fact this was probably not the case—or at any rate not at this stage— because to Communists everywhere the Soviet Army was the sole victor of World War II. Other Allied nations, in their eyes, had played only minor or supporting roles and the Russians had immense military prestige. Soviet officers were considered to be the most advanced strategic and tactical thinkers in the world.

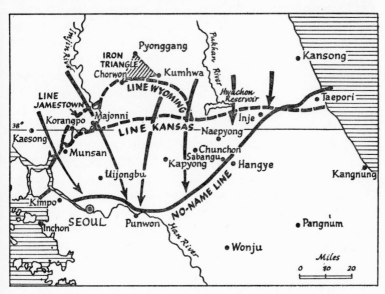

8. COMMUNIST GAINS: APRIL–MAY 1951

Only twelve months previously, a large Soviet Military Mission, with a strength of over 3,000 officers, had arrived in China and was in the process of reorganizing and re-training Mao Tse-tung's army. Accordingly, it is more than probable that the Soviet Military Mission retained the overriding say on how the war in Korea was to be conducted.

If this supposition is correct it is worth remarking that it was out of character for Soviet strategists to favour mass infantry assaults. Although Soviet formations in battle were much closer knit than corresponding ones in Western armies, Soviet military doctrine was based on mobility and fire power and much emphasis was placed on professional and technical skill. Stalin had a poor opinion of guerrilla armies. In Korea the Soviet advisers perhaps agreed to the use of massed infantry because there was no other expedient and, because they were unfamiliar with any other means, Chinese commanders were allowed to fight battles in their own way. However, as more modern material arrived in the country, Soviet influence on its use became more pronounced. Soviet material aid had been trickling through to the CPVA very slowly, being confined at first to motor vehicles and small arms, but it is thought that this policy was deliberate. The Soviet Military Mission was probably unwilling to put complicated arms and vehicles into unskilled hands. Training was stepped up, however, and, during March, large numbers of artillery pieces were received by CPVA formations.

When it moved into Korea in late 1950, the CPVA, composed of elements of both the 3rd and 4th Field Armies, was led by General Lin Piao, but there were indications he was not an unfettered Commander. General Chen Yi, the commander of the 3rd Field Army, was present for part of the time in Korea, overseeing, and probably commanding, the troops from his own formation; but Communist generals were accustomed to 'dual command' and 'command by committee' so this was not quite the drawback that it would have been in a Western expeditionary force.

In March 1951, General Lin Piao was removed from command of the CPVA. It never became clear whether this was because of ill-health, wounds or because he had incurred official Chinese or Soviet displeasure. It may simply have been that he was treated like any other unsuccessful general the world over; or he may have fallen foul of the Soviet military advisers. He was replaced by General Peng Teh-huai, also a veteran general and survivor of the Long March, who when commanding the 1st Field Army had completed the clearing and consolidation of north-west China. Years before, he had served with the Nationalists under Chiang Kai-shek until defecting to the Communists. After the Long March he had commanded the 'Yenan Army' (later to become the 1st Field Army), which had guarded the north-west border region, where Mao Tse-tung had schemed and dreamed for so long. Close to Mao Tse-tung, General Peng had become Deputy Commander of the PLA during the civil war, and he came to the CPVA as a man of immense authority and experience, both political and military, and from the date of his arrival Chinese influence on the strategy of the war increased.

It was estimated that there were about 850,000 Communist troops in Korea at this juncture, of which some 100,000 or more were North Korean. About half were concentrated and committed to the offensive, which had the object of destroying UN forces in the country, and it was rumoured that the Communists were planning to re-take Seoul as a May Day present for Stalin. Of the 70 or so Communist divisions south of the Yalu River, about 15 were grouped in the west between Munsan and the Iron Triangle, about 30 in the area of the Iron Triangle and as far as the Hwachon Reservoir, with about 12 more between the reservoir and the Sea of Japan, the remainder being in reserve.

After a four-hour artillery barrage that surprised the UN intelligence services by its intensity, on the evening of 22nd April, Communist forces moved into the offensive, using at least 15 divisions in the first wave, with as many more in the one which followed a few steps behind. The main weight was directed against I and IX Corps in the west guarding the vulnerable approaches to Seoul but there was also a lesser push in the centre against ROK troops near Inje. Using bugles and flares to co-ordinate the assaults, and gongs and whistles to cause confusion and alarm, supported by mortar and machine-gun fire, Communist soldiers swarmed in to attack UN positions. Small units sought to infiltrate through the UN lines.

CPVA troops forded the Imjin River between Korangpo and Majonni, and another force thrust down along the Chorwon–

Seoul road. The UN line momentarily held firm against this initial shock except in the centre where the CPVA struck at a ROK division that lay between I Corps and IX Corps, scattering part of it and forcing the rest to withdraw. This was a shrewdly chosen weak link and its destruction left a dangerous gap. Formations on either side had to move to prevent themselves from being outflanked. By daybreak (the 23rd), it was obvious that the CPVA was in motion across the breadth of the peninsula, but Chinese soldiers broke contact in their customary manner and, using camouflage and cover, lay low during the daylight hours to avoid artillery and aerial retribution. But in the evening the attack steam-rollered its way forward again, this time jolting US divisions from their positions. The objective seemed to be a double envelopment of Seoul from the north and north-east, the main drive being down the Chorwon–Uijongbu corridor. This time, although the Communist troops still relied mainly upon small arms, grenades and ample use of mortars, increased supporting artillery fire was employed, although not very skilfully.

Left holding a front of about 12,000 yards along the Imjin River was the 29th British Independent Brigade[1] which had been attacked by three CPVA divisions on the first night, but had held fast. The assault was resumed on the second night, but this formation again stood firm despite the weight hurled against it, even though to its south it was being outflanked, as a ROK division was driven back by an enemy thrust down the Kaesong–Munsan route into Seoul. Pressure on the British brigade increased and the Belgian battalion attached to it was evacuated south of the Imjin River. As the Chinese forces crept nearer, one of the British units, the Gloucesters, withdrew to a small hill, known as Point 235, where during the third night of the battle (the 24th) it was surrounded. That night the brigade was ordered to break off the action and move south towards

---

[1] The 29th British Independent Brigade, about 6,000 strong, consisted of the 1st Battalion Northumberland Fusiliers, the 1st Battalion Gloucestershire Regiment and the 1st Battalion Royal Ulster Rifles, with some tanks of the 8th Hussars and other supporting elements. Also attached was the Belgian Battalion.

Seoul to conform to the movement of the whole UN line in this sector, and most elements succeeded in fighting their way back through CPVA ambushes. All, that is, except the Gloucesters who were trapped on their feature, and overrun. This stand on the Imjin River by a British formation in the face of over-whelming odds was one of the epics of the Korean War. It blocked the advance of the Communists for over three days, stopped the momentum of the offensive and protected the left flank of I Corps, thus making an orderly UN withdrawal possible.

Chinese soldiers, relentlessly moving forward in spite of heavy casualties, caused UN formations to give way under the superior weight of manpower. To preserve his front intact, on the 25th General Van Fleet decided to establish a defensive line in the eastern sector which roughly ran from Seoul along the north bank of the Han River. This meant a withdrawal of up to 25 miles in some cases, but it gave him a chance to improve the positioning of his divisions. UN forces formed a covering screen a few miles to the north of Seoul, while armour and artillery were packed into the outskirts of the city ready to make the battle for the South Korean capital a bitter and costly one for the Communists.

Once the Kaesong–Seoul road was cut, the CPVA threw its full weight into this area against Seoul, but the covering screen managed to hold firm. The critical day was the 27th, when Communist forces were again halted. Slightly to the east, the other British formation, the 27th British Commonwealth Brigade, was in action too, successfully checking the CPVA advances near Kapyong; but it was unable to prevent the enemy from cutting the lateral road between Kapyong and Chunchon. The Chinese forces made several further attempts to penetrate the UN-held northern bank of the Han River in the area of Punwon. The next day (the 28th) CPVA assaults were made with failing strength but they still made some gains. As Uijongbu was outflanked, a UN division had to be pulled back almost to within four miles of Seoul. At the same time, ROK troops in the western sector were forced back into the outskirts of the capital by CPVA troops pushing down from the direction of Munsan. To the east, Inje had been taken by the Communists, but further outflanking moves were blocked. On the 29th, UN air strikes broke up an attempt to ferry about 6,000 Chinese soldiers southwards over the Han Estuary into the Kimpo Peninsula to advance on Seoul from the west. This was the last major aggressive move in this offensive and Seoul was safe for the time being. By next day the offensive had clearly run itself out, and a Chinese withdrawal movement was under way. The CPVA had been firmly held short of Seoul and the Han River. This enabled General Van Fleet to bring the UN Forces into a stronger and more favourable defensive line that ran from Seoul to Sabangu, and since this had not been given a name, it was called the No Name Line.

Using their customary tactics, the CPVA had made gains of up to 35 miles but at a cost of over 80,000 casualties. The pattern had been the same as before, with the CPVA divisions able to fight and move continuously for a short period until their food and ammunition were completely exhausted, when they had to withdraw quickly in the face of UN fire power. This time the mobile period had been slightly longer—some seven to eight days instead of the former five to six—but the result had been the same. When they reached the point when they could go on no longer they halted and withdrew. The only notable feature of Chinese tactics was that this time much more artillery had been used. Otherwise, it had been the familiar 'massed' infantry night attacks, the maximum use being made of small arms and mortars, with a pause in the daylight hours while taking cover from superior UN fire, bombs, rockets and napalm. On the UN side morale was high, the much-vaunted CPVA having been held and fought to a standstill. Chinese Communist soldiers no longer appeared supermen—they were simply troops extremely vulnerable to UN fire. UN casualties were only about 7,000—less than one-tenth of those of the enemy.

Both sides now paused for almost a fortnight—the CPVA because it had again outrun its supplies and because most of the divisions committed to battle had suffered heavy casualties; the UN force because it was decided to strengthen the No Name Line to counter a further Communist offensive that was expected in the fairly near future.

General Peng had a massive series of problems which involved not only replenishing his food and ammunition for another offensive, but of changing over all his divisions, marshalling those not yet committed into readiness for the next offensive and moving those shattered by battle to the rear. It was Communist practice that when a formation received heavy casualties or a severe defeat it was disbanded and its personnel were posted to other units. It was not made up to strength with reinforcements, as is usual in the West. It is argued by Chinese military experts that this is a better solution since defeated formations inevitably have an acute morale problem. It is better, they say, to throw in fresh formations at once. They also quickly scatter, and 'brain wash' if necessary soldiers of defeated or demoralized units rather than keep them together with the consequent risk of their fear festering and spreading.

General Van Fleet spent several days fortifying his No Name Line, bringing up guns, planting minefields, erecting barbed wire obstacles, setting gasoline and napalm containers that could be ignited electrically and fixing other defensive devices. The CPVA had broken contact, leaving a gap of up to 10 miles between the two sides along most of the western part of the front, and into this void probing patrols, some armoured, were sent in considerable numbers. Usually these patrols were able to move forward against little or no opposition, and by 7th May both Uijongbu and Chunchon had been reoccupied by small combined armoured and infantry columns. The Kimpo Peninsula was also cleared. Away to the east, ROK forces were moving slowly forward again towards Kansong from Taepori. On the same day, General Van Fleet issued instructions to advance to the old Line Kansas and to halt there. This movement was started but during the next two or three days UN Forces ran into hardening opposition which slowed them down.

The Chinese Air Force became an increasingly important

factor as more modern aircraft were received from the Soviet Union and more Chinese pilots were trained. It was estimated that by May 1951 the Chinese possessed about 1,000 aircraft, and there was evidence that work was rapidly going ahead in the construction of landing-strips in many parts of North Korea. So far Communist aircraft made only brief appearances over the battle zone, but clashes with UN aircraft became more frequent, especially in the north. Whenever the UN air forces made raids near the Yalu River, Chinese planes took off from their bases in Manchuria to intercept. In these aerial conflicts the ratio of 'kills' was roughly 10 to 1 in the UN favour, which it more or less remained for the rest of the war. For example, a large raid by some 300 UN fighter-bombers took place on 9th May, in which an air base at Sinuiju was largely demolished, and in which 15 MiGs were destroyed. Since February, B-29s (Superfortresses) had been meeting MiG opposition and only a month previously (April 1951) 120 UN aircraft on a similar mission were attacked by some 80 MiGs, and in the combat three B-29s were lost for nine MiGs brought down. That was the developing pattern.

During this lull between the two Communist offensives, the UN air forces were heavily engaged in an interdiction role against the many supply columns moving south, both by day when invariably they were resting and by night when they were on the move. They also came into action against the large troop concentrations and movements that were taking place. The UN air forces used a technique of dropping 'para-demolition' bombs, with delayed fuses, descending by parachute at a slow rate to obtain maximum destruction. These did not rebound or cannon off the target, as fast falling bombs tended to do, and were particularly effective against bridges.

Meanwhile, feverish preparations were being made by the CPVA to mount another offensive and fresh divisions were being marched rapidly southwards towards the fighting areas. At the same time, partly to cause a diversion and partly in a major attempt to force a wedge between the UN X Corps and the ROK troops, Communist forces, starting on 10th May, began to infiltrate through the eastern mountains in the region of Inje. All along the front there was a sharp increase in the number of Communist agents slipping across the lines, always an indication that an attack was imminent. Having deployed some 20 fresh CPVA divisions in the forward areas, mainly in the central sector, General Peng was at last ready to launch them against the UN Forces that were still trying to move cautiously northwards. Three of the available North Korean divisions, none of which had suffered in the last offensive to the same degree as those of the CPVA, were put on the western flank, and six on the eastern one. More divisions were positioned to follow up, and in all about 300,000 Communist troops were about to be committed to battle.

After an artillery barrage on the night of 15th/16th May, the second Communist offensive of this phase of the war began. Heavy pressure was applied in the eastern sector, where about 12 divisions were concentrated between Naepyong and the coast and the spearhead hit two ROK divisions of X Corps near Hangye. These two formations gave way and enemy troops rushed into the gap, obliging the UN forces on either side to fall back. X Corps had to try to move units to the east to hold the sagging line. North Korean soldiers exploited the situation, and during the next two or three days they made advances of up to 50 miles, until they were finally halted just north of the road from Kangnung to Pangnum. In the centre a similar tussle was in progress in which the US Marine Division and a ROK one blocked Communist attacks, especially in the area of the Chunchon plain. The French and Dutch Battalions were heavily engaged in this fighting, the difficulties of which were increased by the necessity of moving formations away to help in the eastern sector. While the struggle in the east and the centre was in progress, on the 17th three CPVA divisions struck southwards down the Pukhan River towards the Han River, but after three days' combat this thrust was held by a US and a ROK division. Another weaker diversionary stab, made in the west against Seoul, was more easily checked by ROK units.

By the 20th, the Communist offensive had spent its force and its momentum had run down because, after the usual short period of fighting, this time between five and six days, it had exhausted its supplies and ammunition. Only comparatively small territorial gains had been made in return for staggering losses. It was estimated that in those few days the Communists had suffered about 120,000 casualties, from napalm, bombing, artillery and small-arms fire. Communist tactics had been on much the usual pattern—mass infantry assaults by night, heavy use of small-arms, grenades and mortars, backed by more artillery this time, with pauses during daylight to avoid UN aerial and artillery attention. The plain fact was that the Communist offensive had been halted by the fire power of the UN forces, and this for the second time within six weeks. These two unsuccessful all-out offensives which had cost over 200,000 casualties, approximately one-third of the Communist force involved, had shown the Communists that their chances of winning the war by committing their troops to battle in mass were poor. The myth of the invincible Chinese guerrilla was dissolving fast.

Even before the Communist offensive had run down, General Van Fleet had already, on the 18th, started his counter-offensive, instructing I Corps, in the west, to move forward, which it did by making a series of local attacks to clear the ground in front of the UN line. His aim was to prevent the CPVA reorganizing to attack in strength again, to threaten the supply route into the Hwachow Reservoir area, and then to assault and capture the Iron Triangle. The first stage was to regain Line Kansas and, although handicapped by a shortage of ammunition, especially for the artillery because so much had been expended in the recent fighting, by the 29th UN forces were again moving northwards across the width of the peninsula in the wake of retreating Communist soldiers. By the 27th, elements of X Corps had reoccupied Inje. Next, Kansong, on the east coast, was taken by ROK forces.

Communist military resistance had virtually collapsed and the UN line moved northwards fairly fast, being handicapped only by lack of ammunition and transport and the problem of distributing supplies in such difficult terrain. General Van Fleet wanted the UN line to remain intact and did not allow any deep salients that might easily be enveloped. By 1st June Line Kansas had been reached in most parts, and the Joint Chiefs of Staff ordered Van Fleet to halt his troops. The area was cleared of civilians and work started to fortify it, deep shelters being constructed with strong overhead cover as protection against Communist artillery fire.

The decision to halt at Line Kansas, or on such parts as had been reached, instead of pursuing the retreating Communist troops, is one over which there was controversy. From a military point of view it was a wrong one, as the CPVA was disorganized, demoralized and on the run, a situation that should have been exploited to the full. For the first time, Chinese soldiers were surrendering in large numbers, over 17,000 doing so in the last fortnight of May. It was obvious that the UN forces were not numerous enough to move deep into North Korea and encircle the nearly one million Communist troops there and sensible strategy decreed that a continuous line across the peninsula should be maintained. Nevertheless this line could have been advanced well into North Korea. It is true this would have posed problems of communication and supply, but these would not have been insurmountable. Every day of delay gave the CPVA time to recover and there can be no doubt that the decision to halt on Line Kansas was an unfortunate one. Physical occupation of a large section of North Korea would have had immense value at any negotiating table. Military decisions must be made within the terms of a political brief but, here again, there were divided opinions. The prevailing political view was that it would be best to halt to feel out Chinese intentions, for it was hoped that they would realize they were beaten in the field and so would be eager to negotiate. After a few days, when there was no sign of any Communist overtures, General Van Fleet ordered I and IX Corps to advance to Line Wyoming, to iron out the bulge that ran from the Imjin River, through Chorwon and Kumhwa to the Hwachon Reservoir. Grudgingly, the Joint Chiefs of Staff in Washington allowed the UN forces to move northwards and to cross the 38th Parallel.

There was still only spasmodic although sometimes surprisingly prickly resistance, but by 11th June Chorwon had been taken by US, ROK and Philippine troops. On the same day, US units and the Turkish Brigade seized Kumhwa. Other local advances were made to secure better defensive positions. Still advancing, UN troops entered the empty shell of Pyongyang, the North Korean capital, on the 13th, but as it was dominated by hills infested with Communist soldiers they were ordered to evacuate, thus allowing the CPVA to take possession again on the 17th. By mid-June, the advance having come to a halt on orders from the Joint Chiefs of Staff, the UN line across Korea, which now included both Chorwon and Kumhwa, was stabilized. Attention was given to establishing strong defensive positions. Generally there was little activity along its length, except in the area that came to be known as the Punch Bowl, a narrow depression amid mountain ridges and peaks to the north of Inje, where some violent battles were fought.

The decision to halt the UN advance at this stage was certainly wrong from a military point of view, since the CPVA was still in poor condition and had only limited defensive capabilities. Despite heavy rains that restricted air support and turned roads and valleys into morasses, the UN forces could have pushed on several more miles with little difficulty before hardening resistance slowed them down.

By this time, high hopes had arisen in the West that the war in Korea was virtually over. Both the UN and the USA hoped that restraint and a lull in operations might produce an atmosphere conducive to bringing about a cease-fire and on 23rd June Jacob Malik, the Soviet delegate to the UN, proposed a discussion between the participants in Korea. This was the first positive peace reaction from the Communist camp. Shortly afterwards, Peking radio indicated that China favoured a truce, and on President Truman's authority, General Ridgway was allowed to open negotiations with enemy generals.

CHAPTER 9

The Long Stalemate

After the first year of the war in Korea, which ended with the defeat of the Communist forces in the field, there followed two more of dragging stalemate during which protracted truce negotiations took place. The war of movement ended and no more large offensives were mounted by either side. There were, however, a number of bitter battles fought, mainly for the possession of tactical features along the length of the stabilized and fortified front lines. These flare-ups, which gained little territory but cost many lives, often coincided with the breakdown of truce negotiations. Overhead the air war was intensified.

Official contacts between the combatants resulted in the first meeting of the Truce Delegation on 10th July 1951, at Kaesong, which was about three miles south of the 38th Parallel and was believed by the UN forces to be in 'no-man's-land'. In fact it was dominated by the Communists, which made for difficulties. The UN Truce Delegation was led by Vice-Admiral C. Turner Joy, the US Far East Naval Commander, and consisted of three other senior US officers and Major-General Paik Sun Yup, representing South Korea. The Communist Delegation, led by Lieutenant-General Nam Il, of North Korea, also consisted of five members, the others being two senior North Korean officers and two Chinese generals. Already, on 1st February 1951, the UN had declared Communist China to be an aggressor in Korea.

Both sides agreed that hostilities would continue until a truce was signed, and the first sessions were devoted to hammering out technicalities, such as demarcation lines, routes to the truce negotiations centre, Press facilities and settling the agenda. Little progress was made since from the start it was obvious that the Communist Delegation was being deliberately obstructive, was playing for time and angling for attention and prestige. Negotiations were abruptly broken off in August.

The opposing UN and Communist front lines now spread from coast to coast, and both sides began feverishly to improve, strengthen and fortify them. Over the next few months each attempted to acquire desirable tactical features to benefit their defences, which resulted in a number of battles in the late summer and autumn, mainly at the base of the Iron Triangle. There was heavy fighting as X Corps and ROK troops sought to improve their positions north and east of the Hwachon Reservoir, and towards the Punch Bowl area. In July, after a four-day battle, they took a key peak, Taeusan (Hill 1179), but shortly afterwards Bloody Ridge (Hill 983) in the same complex was lost. Bloody Ridge changed hands several times during September. By the 18th, US Marines were consolidating to the north of the Punch Bowl. The fighting continued until 14th October, by which time both Bloody Ridge and Heart-Break Ridge (Hill 931) were in UN hands.

Elsewhere heavy UN pressure was maintained to improve the defence line against increasing Communist resistance and artillery fire. For example, by 21st October a US division succeeded in taking some heights above Kumsong, which were about 20 miles north of the 38th Parallel. This more or less completed General Van Fleet's immediate plans, which had been to advance to a line known as Jamestown. On 12th November General Ridgway ordered that there should be no more offensive action, but instead UN troops were to carry out an 'active defence'. No more attacks involving more than one battalion in size were to be made unless express permission was given. The Main Line of Resistance, the MLR as it came to be known, was now established, and ran for 155 miles. It was held by three US and one ROK corps, which from west to east were I, IX and X Corps and the ROK I Corps.

Reinforcements from America enabled US formations that had been in combat for a long time either to be relieved or brought into reserve for a rest and refit.[1] The first National Guard division arrived in Korea in December (1951) and replaced the 1st Cavalry Division. The second National Guard division arrived the following month, enabling General Van Fleet to redeploy his forces to give ROK troops a greater share in the defence. On 28th July (1951) the 1st Commonwealth

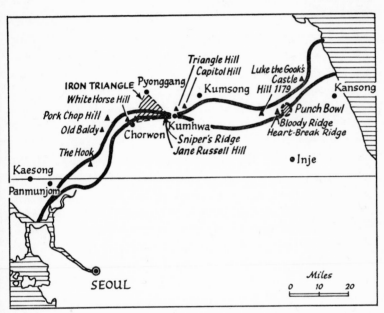

9. MAIN LINE OF RESISTANCE

Division was formed from British and Commonwealth formations and units serving in Korea.

To the north, the Communists were also busily engaged in replacing and redeploying divisions, and the main feature of these changes was that all North Korean forces were regrouped in the eastern sector, where they were brought face to face with ROK troops.

With the advent of military ground stalemate the need for

[1] In August 1951, when the MLR stabilized there were about 586,000 troops in the UN Command, of which 229,000 were American.

close air support in the field was considerably reduced, so a new UN strategy, one of large-scale interdiction, was substituted. The object of Operation Strangle, as this air offensive was known, was to sever the Communist forward zone from the rest of North Korea. It was estimated that about 60 (of the 90) Communist divisions in North Korea were in the forward zone, and that they required, as a minimum, 3,000 tons of supplies daily. Of this tonnage, about half was brought south by rail, and the remainder by trucks and porters. Thousands of North Koreans were conscripted for this purpose, and by using the native A-frame[1] they were each able to carry a 45-lb load for 12 miles overnight. For obvious reasons, Communist supplies moved mainly under cover of darkness.

There had been a large influx of Soviet trucks into North Korea in the first half of 1951, and they were primarily used for supply purposes. It was thought they had increased from about 7,300 in January to over 55,000 by June, so it was decided to concentrate first of all upon trying to interdict the road system. Increasing their strikes to about 700 sorties a day during July, UN aircraft taking part in Operation Strangle rained down bombs on the roads of North Korea. But the roads were repaired almost as quickly as they were damaged by conscripted labour, and by the end of the month just as many Communist trucks laden with supplies were rolling south as before.

During the next month, August, Operation Strangle was broadened to include the railway system as well as the roads, and in particular bridges were attacked. The idea was to damage or cut both road and rail communications at intervals of about one mile, so that it would mean maximum dispersion of the Communist labour gangs. Also, it meant a greater dispersal of anti-aircraft weapons, which were being received in larger numbers from the Soviet Union, and a corresponding lessening of density of hostile fire against UN aircraft. Communist air defences were improving rapidly as Soviet equipment

[1] The Korean 'A-frame' was a contraption, somewhat in the shape of the letter A, fitting on to the back, enabling loads to be carried more comfortably.

arrived, which included radar-controlled anti-aircraft guns and searchlights. The Communists in North Korea became experts at dispersion, deception, and camouflage. Trains were kept in tunnels in daylight and trucks in caves by the roadside or disguised as native huts. Straw aircraft were put on dummy airfields, and good airfields were camouflaged to appear riddled with craters and completely unusable. Also, many dummy installations, factories, camps and barracks were set up to deflect UN attention. Generally, the US Air Force concentrated upon the western side of Korea, and the US Naval Air Force on the eastern part, both being co-ordinated from a Joint Operations Centre in Seoul. Naval aircraft flew from such ships as the USN Carriers *Antietam* and *Valley Forge*, floating off-shore in the Sea of Japan.

Almost overnight a powerful Chinese air force had materialized to threaten that of the UN. In May 1951, it was estimated there were about 400 MiG-15s (out of the probable 1,000 or so aircraft) all based in Manchuria and China, but by the following May this number had grown to at least 1,000 jets. Operating from such bases as Antung, and others in the Mukden area, MiGs would fly over the Yalu River in mass; and while some sorties were directed to the Wonsan and Chinampo regions, and others penetrated well south—some even as far as Seoul—the majority stayed over the area between the Yalu and Chongchon Rivers, which became known as 'MiG Alley'. Once this pattern was grasped, the UN air forces left their F-86s (Sabre Jets) to battle with the MiGs, withdrawing other types of fighters and interceptors—such as the Gloster Meteors flown by the 77th Australian Squadron, RAAF—south of the Chongchon River for patrol and escort duties. The F-86 (Sabre Jet), with six .50-inch machine-guns, was the only UN interceptor that could stand up to the MiG-15, which had a 37-mm and two 20-mm cannons. At the end of 1951, another F-86 (Sabre Jet) group, based on Suwon, was formed to assist the hard-worked and hard-pressed US 4th Fighter Interceptor Group based on Kimpo airfield.

Communist air activity increased sharply in the latter part of

1951 rising to about 3,700 jet aircraft sorties in January (1952). Then it declined just as steeply to 308 jet aircraft sorties in June. The main reason was because the standard of training and the ability of the Chinese pilots was not equal to those of the Americans'. Precious jet aircraft were not to be lightly risked; and they were still being shot down by UN interceptors in a ratio of about 10 to 1.

During September 1951 it became apparent that a major programme to complete a network of some 34 jet airfields in North Korea was under way, and that at least three, near villages called Saamcham, Taechon and Namsi, near the Chongchon River, were well advanced. If these airfields were available for staging and refuelling MiGs it could mean dangerously increased opposition to the UN air forces. By mid-October the Saamcham and Taechom airfields were disrupted by UN raids, in which only one B-29 (Superfortress) was lost. On October 23rd a force of B-29s, with a fighter escort, moved to strike at Namsi, but was met by a swarm of about 150 MiGs. In the ensuing battle, three B-29s were shot down and five others damaged. In the course of the next few days, more large swarms of MiGs crossed the Yalu River daily into MiG Alley to attack any UN aircraft they encountered. This caused several UN losses. Although still not venturing much farther south than the Chongchon River, the Chinese air force became such a menace that the UN forces were compelled to suspend daylight bombing raids over North Korea. Instead, using radar and 'Shoran' (Short Range Navigation), a system of electronic beam navigation, the B-29s, flying by night, concentrated upon disrupting Communist airfields under construction.

There was also activity at sea by the warships from several nations that went to make up the UN naval forces. Their main task was to blockade the North Korean coast; targets along the coastline were bombarded; at times a rocket-firing landing ship was used. Continuous naval sieges were maintained at Wonsan, Hungnam and Songjin, but no amphibious landings were made. It was felt that large amphibious landings might tend to cool the climate to below the level necessary for successful truce talks. Apart from blockade tasks the ships of the UN naval force were engaged in perpetual mine warfare, dealing with both magnetic and contact mines sown by the Communists.

Negotiations—broken off on 23rd August because a UN aircraft was alleged to have violated neutral air-space—were resumed on 25th October, this time at Panmunjom, about five miles east of Kaesong, but they did not produce any results and were almost immediately suspended. This rupture of the truce talks coincided with an outbreak of ground fighting in places along the by now very well fortified MLR. By June 1952[1] negotiations, which had been briefly resumed, again reached a deadlock, this time over prisoners of war. It was obvious that the Communists were playing for time and that peace was no nearer, so the UN Command brought a new aerial strategy into operation. In January (1952) the UN air forces had alternated daily with massed artillery to pulverize the enemy near the front line, and while this undoubtedly discouraged and hampered offensive action and gave a demonstration of UN fire power, its only practical effect had been to force the Communist soldiers to dig in deeper. Up-country, Operation Strangle was doing no better, and by spring it was becoming obvious that aerial interdiction alone, without ground offensive action, was unable to stop the Communists from supplying their forward formations, despite the almost 100 per cent use of the UN air power available.

So far, Operation Strangle had failed in its objective. The chief cause of the failure was the fact that the source of raw materials and the main factories were beyond the Yalu River where they were secure from UN aerial attack. Another major cause was the Communist development of a highly organized system of forced labour which enabled both the roads and the railways to be repaired at once by gangs that were largely immune to attacks as they lived, or sheltered, in caves alongside

---

[1] In May 1952, Major-General William K. Harrison succeeded Admiral Joy as Chief UN Delegate.

the stretch of road or railway they were responsible for, and where there was always ample natural material available for repair work.

Something else had to be tried, and so the Special Targets System was put into operation in June (1952). This simply meant that a large force of bombers was directed at selected vital targets. The first gigantic raid was made on the 23rd, when some 500 UN aircraft struck at the Suiho Hydro Dam, on the Yalu River, about 35 miles from Antung, which supplied electricity to Manchurian industries as well as to North Korea. Built by the Japanese, it was the fourth largest dam in the world. Such North Korean industries as were functioning were dispersed and reasonably secure underground, but they still needed power in order to operate. It is surprising that this target had not been eliminated months before. The next month, on 11th July, there was a daylight raid by some 1,200 UN aircraft on the factory, stores and camp complex that had developed around Pyongyang in which napalm as well as high-explosive bombs were dropped. During the following months, similar massive raids were made on oil refineries, transport centres and industrial installations.

When it was seen that these aerial attacks had no effect on the truce talks, that the damage caused was quickly put right, at least partially, and that repairs could be made which enabled the North Korean economy to function and a large military force to be kept at the front, 'concentrated' raids were tried out. These, aimed at river crossing points, mainly on the Chongchon and Taedong Rivers, were raids that continued without respite for up to five days, the maximum time for which operations such as these could be maintained. This strategy, too, proved a failure since invariably, on the evening of the sixth day, Communists were once again crossing the river, having patched up the broken bridges or improvised in some other way.

In February (1953)[1] the Suiho Hydro Dam, which had been

---

[1] On 12th January 1953 the Chinese shot down a US B-29 which had strayed over Manchuria, alleging it to be on a 'spy' photographic mission.

partially repaired, was again attacked by a large force of UN aircraft. And so on.

When the truce talks bogged down once more in May 1953, it was decided to strike heavily at five of the twenty major dams in North Korea, a step not taken so far largely on humanitarian grounds. Although repairs were put in hand by the Communists with their usual promptitude, there are indications that this might have been the one really effective aerial policy had it been put into operation months earlier. By the time the war ended, there were fifteen large dams in North Korea still unbombed.

In America the Korean War was one of the main issues of the Presidential election campaign in the autumn of 1952, as was the lack of development of the ROK forces, which had been deliberately neglected. The war was unpopular in the USA, and so in consequence were several of the Truman Administration personalities. In November, Eisenhower was elected President of the United States.

This brought about a change in policy and attitudes towards the Communists, especially in the Far East. Eisenhower had made a pre-election promise to try and end the war in Korea, which he meant to honour if he could and, as President-Elect, he visited that country in December 1952. Whilst there he saw that the small, costly prestige battles along the MLR would never force a military result, and he realized that the American people would not tolerate an indefinite static struggle with such a casualty rate. Syngman Rhee advocated an all-out attack on the Communists as soon as possible, while most of the field commanders seemed to be of the opinion that if fruitless negotiations dragged on there would be no alternative except to resume the offensive. Eisenhower also became aware of certain UN ammunition shortages. There was a general disillusionment on the part of many who had reluctantly come to the conclusion that the Chinese Communists were ruthless aggressors and not, as had been piously hoped, merely 'agrarian reformers' bent only upon doing good. On his return from Korea, Eisenhower said,[1] 'We face an enemy whom we cannot

[1] *Mandate for Change, 1953-56.*

hope to impress by words however eloquent but only by deeds—executed under circumstances of our own choosing.' In his first speech on the State of the Union to Congress, in February (1953), President Eisenhower indicated that the days of the stalemate in Korea must be numbered and gave a hint of the possibility of strong action. He also said that the US 7th Fleet would no longer screen the Chinese mainland from any Nationalist Chinese attack.

General Mark Clark, who had taken over the appointment of CICUNC[1] in May 1952 from General Ridgway, was in favour of a tough policy. Recommending the use of at least two Nationalist Chinese divisions in Korea, he was suspected to be in favour of the use of the atomic bomb and of hitting the source of Communist supplies on the other side of the Yalu River. As Eisenhower had been a general too, it was expected he would have more practical sympathy with such recommendations than Truman.

General Clark had just obtained permission to increase the ROK Army. His predecessor, General Ridgway, had not been in favour of this and in April (1951) had advised against a projected expansion of the ROK army by ten divisions. He estimated that the ROK equipment losses in the first ten months of the war had been the equivalent of 'ten divisions' worth', some of which had been abandoned without a fight. Like MacArthur, Ridgway had been of the opinion that the ROK standard of officer leadership and training should be considerably improved first. An additional fear had no doubt been that, if given extra arms, Syngman Rhee would distribute them to his youth organizations and so develop armed political units. But now the emphasis changed. Syngman Rhee got his way at last and a programme of ROK Army expansion belatedly began. President Eisenhower, impressed by what he had seen of the ROK Army in Korea, had given authority to

[1] General Clark was also the Commander-in-Chief Far East Command, over all US forces in that theatre. The title Supreme Commander Allied Powers had been dropped when the Japanese peace treaty became effective on 28th April 1952.

assist it to increase from 460,000 to 525,000, and two new divisions began to form.

Meanwhile spasmodic ground fighting continued all along the MLR, taking the form of tussles for tactical features that occasionally developed into battles, skirmishes, patrol actions and small raids to obtain information or take prisoners. Prestige flare-ups frequently followed a breakdown in negotiations. The UN casualties for each of the two years of this stalemate amounted to over 30,000, and as it was a case of Communist manpower against UN fire power, enemy casualties were many times greater.

The Communists constructed a fortified belt, at least 15 miles and up to 25 miles deep in places, the individual positions and posts being well dug in and having stout overhead protection many feet thick. Obviously they had in mind the possibility that nuclear weapons might be used against them. The actual defensive positions were usually sited on reverse slopes, a tactic forced on them by inferior fire power. They were literally underground fortresses, tunnelling deep into the mountain sides so that no Chinese troops were left out in the open and they had ample manpower to do this the hard way. Large numbers of guns had been received and, at the end of 1951, they were beginning to spout barrages. The guns themselves were drawn from the tunnels by manpower to fire and were then quickly pushed back again. The Communists improved their artillery battle techniques and became able to concentrate up to 12 guns on a target and to carry out reasonably efficient counter-bombardment. Their guns were also deeply dug in, and did not move from their positions to give close support to the infantry when it assaulted. In the attack, the infantry had to rely for supporting fire mainly upon mortars, of which by this time there were plenty. The chief Communist problem—the result of UN air activity—was that of ammunition supply, and they were never able to use fire power as lavishly as the UN forces. The CPVA also had a small number of tanks but these did not figure largely in any of the battles.

By the end of 1952, Communist forces in North Korea amounted to about 1.2 million, of which about one million were Chinese. The effective commander was still General Peng, who had brought his influence to bear on strategy. There were about 270,000 soldiers in the MLR, formed into seven Chinese armies and two North Korean corps. In the rear, and in support, were about another 531,000 troops, distributed in eleven Chinese armies and one North Korean corps. The remainder, about 400,000, were employed on logistic tasks—another point for those inclined to think that Communist soldiers are all front-line fighters. In addition, over one million North Koreans were conscripted to repair communications or as porters.

The UN forces in Korea had risen to a total of 768,000, including logistic troops. The combat elements consisted of 16 divisions in the MLR (4 American, 1 Commonwealth and 11 ROK) and another four in reserve (3 American and 1 ROK). The UN line was not so strong and deeply entrenched as that of the Communists, and consisted of a continuous bunkered-trench defensive system, with a secondary one to back it up in places. The pattern of defence was for the forward UN defensive positions to be sited on the forward slopes, so as to be able to make the best of superior fire power, with deep shelters for personnel to move to in rotation on the reverse slopes. In August (1952) the Korean Communications Zone was formed with the primary purpose of relieving the 8th Army of the responsibilities for rear areas, logistic support, prisoners and the civil population.

Both defensive lines were so strong that neither side could make major moves forward without incurring huge losses. The possibility was examined occasionally, especially when the Communists deliberately broke off truce talks, of whether the UN Forces should mount an all-out offensive that would smash through the Communist defensive belt and advance well into North Korea. Each time this course was rejected, mainly on the grounds that it could only succeed at a very heavy cost in casualties. Also, the existing MLR had a good tactical defensive capability that probably could not be bettered any farther north.

Typical of the several tussles for tactical features that developed into prestige battles was that for White Horse Hill (Hill 395), which was fought towards the end of 1952. This was started by the Communists on 6th October, when they assaulted the feature, held by ROK troops, and on the next day over 93,000 shells fell on UN forces in this area, which was just to the west of the Iron Triangle. Ten days' bitter fighting followed in which the ROK formation retained the position and a CPVA division was decimated. As a diversion, on the 14th, a UN Task Force mounted an attack at the other end of the Iron Triangle apex, near Kumhwa, where Communist outposts overlooked the UN line. Despite air and artillery support this did not succeed as the enemy was too well dug in. This became a separate prestige action as more troops were thrown into the fight which lasted for about a fortnight. When the battle died down, the UN forces had gained a tiny foothold at one corner of the Iron Triangle, holding part of two features, both of dubious tactical value, known as Sniper's Ridge and Jane Russell Hill. The cost of this minute advance had been about 8,000 UN casualties, but over 12,000 had been inflicted on the enemy, whose commanders, as usual, showed an apparent disregard for the lives of their soldiers in battle. Several other battles of a similar nature were fought over such features known as The Hook, Triangle Hill, Capitol Hill, Luke the Gook's Castle and Old Baldy.

During the opening months of 1953, ground activity along the MLR was reduced to patrol actions and small raids,[1] but spring brought a resurgence of Communist assaults, some involving divisional strength or more. On 16th April, the Communists attacked Pork Chop Hill, part of a hill complex about 12 miles west of Chorwon, and the battle ebbed and flowed over it. Pork Chop Hill became a prestige position, with each side throwing in more and more troops. This see-saw

---

[1] On 11th February 1953, Lieutenant-General Maxwell D. Taylor took over the command of the 8th Army from General Van Fleet.

fighting continued until 12th July, when UN troops decided to withdraw. Once more heavy casualties had been fruitlessly incurred.

Communist assaults were also aimed at ROK formations, which manned about 75 per cent of the length of the MLR, and and on 13th June, in one of the last actions of the war, the enemy broke through the UN defence line where ROK troops were holding it on the right flank of IX Corps. One ROK division collapsed under the pressure, and three others were badly mauled. US troops were moved up and a new defence line on the Kumsong River was stabilized. A counter-attack by three ROK divisions began on the 16th, aiming at straightening out the bulge made by the Communists. It recovered some ground and UN fire power caused Communist casualties. This offensive had faded out by the 20th.

Although the war was predominantly fought with American money, material and troops, South Korean susceptibilities had to be considered and the façade of South Korean independence supported to the full. As President Syngman Rhee had a mind of his own and his aims did not always coincide with those of the UN or the USA, at times the American Government found him difficult. Personifying the stand of South Korea against Communist aggression, there was no doubt that he was a popular leader who stood head and shoulders above any of his countrymen. He had the support of the army, which often took orders direct from him, the police, the civil service, the nationalist organizations and the bulk of the people. He was single-minded in his view that Korea should be a united country, and he disapproved of the truce negotiations.[1] In this he came into conflict with the UN and America, which were all for ending the war as soon as possible and were not prepared any longer to fight on to gain North Korea by force of arms. It was because he not only stood up to the Communists but also to the UN and the USA whenever he thought they were over-riding South Korean interests, that his popularity increased amongst all the non-Communist sections within his country.

[1] Chiang Kai-shek also loudly urged there should be a time limit.

While there had been little hope of negotiations bearing fruit, Syngman Rhee had been passive towards them but once the prospects of a truce became brighter, he used all his political acumen to prevent an armistice being signed.

Syngman Rhee was by then 78 years old and many secretly hoped that his advanced age would compel him before long to quit politics; but they were disappointed. In August 1952 he was re-elected President with a huge majority. Secure in the support of his countrymen, he demanded to be allowed to move his Government back to Seoul. General Clark refused to permit this but, ignoring the ban, Syngman Rhee moved to Seoul from Pusan with his personal staff, and his Ministries followed him there one by one. Perhaps the biggest rupture in his relations with the UN and the US occurred on 18th July 1953, when Syngman Rhee ordered the release of over 25,000 anti-Communist prisoners and detainees held in South Korean camps, so that they would not be handed over to the Communists in any negotiated agreement, which at that moment seemed possible. This was a deliberate act designed to foil any truce. The next day he released 2,000 more. The American Government was furious; and to make matters worse, instead of being penitent and grateful for American military aid without which he would not have been in his office and position, he threatened to withdraw his South Korean troops from the UN Command. For a few days the question of whether or not the war could continue hung in the balance.

Sometime either later in March or in April (1953) the Communists decided to end the war, a decision arrived at for two reasons. The first was the fear that America was fast losing patience and was about to use nuclear weapons. The other was the death of Stalin.

President Eisenhower, worried by the continuing heavy casualties, realized that the stalemate must soon be ended one way or another, and several options were seriously considered, including the possibility of a massive UN attack northwards. About this, in his memoirs[1] he wrote 'to keep the attack from

[1] *Mandate for Change, 1953-56.*

becoming overly costly it was clear we would have to use atomic weapons'. His view was that the will to use such means was as important as possessing them. However, he felt that such a course of action would cause a rift with some UN countries, especially Britain, but he thought this could have been repaired in time. In February (1953) it had been deliberately leaked to the Communists that the USA would not be restricted in the use of any weapon it possessed in the war in Korea, and this resulted in a dramatic exchange of prisoners. Signs of US determination to use the bomb should it be necessary became more obvious.

Nuclear weapons had been moved to Okinawa, ready for use either in North Korea, Manchuria or against the Chinese mainland, and this was known to the Communist leaders who, despite the boast of Mao Tse-tung that the atomic bomb was a 'paper tiger', were realists and knew exactly what such an attack would mean. They had no intention of allowing the war to be carried into China. US senior officers had made a secret study of the use of nuclear weapons in Korea and against China, and they knew this too. This Communist decision to accept a truce may have been reinforced when on 1st May (1953) America exploded its first hydrogen bomb. The Soviet Union had still to follow suit, and the Chinese Communists did not know how far behind in the nuclear race that country was. They strongly suspected, too, that it had no intention of joining with China, should it come to open war against America.

Stalin's death, in March 1953, removed a powerful influence from the scene. He had wanted the Korean sore to continue to fester so as to draw Western military strength and attention away from the Cold War in Europe. With Stalin out of the way, Soviet influence on the Korean War lessened, and that of China increased sharply.

The first sign of an approaching agreement was when the Communists responded to UN suggestions that wounded prisoners should be exchanged, and on 9th April a party of British internees was put on a train that eventually carried it to the Soviet Union, and from thence to Britain. This was followed, on the 29th, by 'Little Switch', lasting until 3rd May, when 6,670 Communists were exchanged for 684 UN personnel.

By April, the Chinese Communist leaders had made up their minds and on the 26th a plenary session of the Truce Delegations was held at Panmunjom, the first since the previous October. They bargained long and hard, recessing on 20th June, until 10th July, and it was not until 27th July that an Armistice Agreement, to come into effect that day, was signed.

After lasting for three years, one month and two days, the war in Korea was brought to an end. The country still remained divided, the Armistice line being the positions reached by the forward troops, roughly slightly to the north of the 38th Parallel. In detail, South Korea lost some 850 square miles of territory and had to give up several UN-occupied islands north of the Armistice line, while North Korea lost about 2,350 square miles of its country. There was difficulty in persuading Syngman Rhee, who had done his best to block truce negotiations, to agree to comply with the conditions of the Armistice Agreement, and it was feared he might order the release of many prisoners and thus embarrass the UN Command. His support was bought at a heavy price, which included a mutual security pact with the USA, material assistance to build the ROK Army up to 20 divisions, and a $200-million economic aid programme. On 12th July, Syngman Rhee was persuaded to state publicly that he would co-operate in the truce arrangements.

As is usual in war, the cost in human life, misery and suffering was great, and completely out of proportion to any benefits that may have been gained by the UN or by the Communists. At least 104,430 soldiers of the UN forces (including the ROK) were killed, and over 295,575 wounded. The Communist military casualties were estimated to be 1,347,000 dead and wounded. Civilians suffered heavily—thousands were killed, tens of thousands imprisoned, hundreds of thousands removed from their homes. Both North and South Korea were economically devastated.

CHAPTER 10

The Psycholgoical War

The psychological aspects of the war are very interesting. Probably for the first time in history the Communists deliberately used their personnel captured by UN Forces as a 'sixth column', since they all continued, even though taken prisoner, to work for victory. The custom had been that prisoners of war were *hors de combat*, having merely to be fed and housed under reasonable conditions until hostilities ceased, when they were returned to their own countries. The only moral obligations upon them were that they should not impart any military information to the enemy, and should escape if that were a practical proposition. Brushing aside these traditions, the Communists had great success in manipulating their captured personnel, who rioted, demonstrated and loudly protested to order, at times and on occasions calculated to make the maximum impact on world opinion. This policy was especially effective during the 'negotiation war'.

The first Communist military prisoners captured in battle were placed in small camps around Pusan, and to them were added civilians regarded as potential security risks. These camps hampered communications, so from early in 1951 the prisoners and detainees were shipped to Koje Island, about 30 miles off-shore, where their numbers swelled as more were captured. Specially trained agents allowed themselves to be taken prisoner in the fighting so they would be sent to Koje, where they were able to organize and impose rigid discipline upon the prisoners there. There was an almost constant struggle for supremacy in the compounds between the Communists and anti-Communists, which resulted in many fights and scuffles. Communist courts tried and sentenced prisoners, and Communist terror squads eliminated those who opposed them, the dead being secretly disposed of. Intensive indoctrination was carried out, the situation becoming such in some of the compounds that the guards, of whom five were killed by the prisoners in the first year, dared not venture into them.

Communication between the Communist prison organization on Koje and North Korea was operated through numerous channels, and the inhabitants who had remained on the island assisted. Thus there was a two-way flow of information, and means existed for the passage of orders and instructions from the joint KPA-CPVA GHQ. Lieutenant-General Nam Il, Chief of Staff to the KPA, was credited with organizing and controlling the 'sixth column'.

The first scheme was that the prisoners should prepare to make a sudden mass break-out to join the guerrillas in the hills of South Korea, but when the front line stabilized and truce talks began, this was superseded by other and more workable ideas. Keyed to their obstructive tactics at the negotiating table, the prisoners were to riot and demonstrate to order to embarrass the UN in the eyes of the world and to help the Communist cause. There had in fact been an attempted break-out on 15th August (1951) when nine prisoners were killed, but now the emphasis changed.

However, one Communist tactic backfired. They had demanded that all prisoners be screened to ensure that none were held back by the UN on the pretext that they did not wish to return home again, it being UN policy that no one should be forcibly repatriated against his will. They thought there would be no difficulty and that it would be to their ultimate benefit, but the screening produced results that were dismaying to the Communists. It was found that large numbers did not in fact want to return. Once this was appreciated, the Communist leaders in the prison compounds were ordered to obstruct all screening measures by the UN, to intensify their indoctrination and to establish a firmer hold on the inmates. On 18th February (1952) prison guards who were attacked opened fire, killing about 75 and wounding over 100 prisoners. The Communists made capital from this incident throughout the world at large. 'Shooting defenceless prisoners' is excellent propaganda material. In March and April there were more riots protesting against screening. Although many of the compounds were seething with mutiny and some were almost completely autonomous, the true situation was not understood and in fact its seriousness may not have been fully realized by the higher UN Command. Where it was known, it was played down because it might have had an adverse effect on the truce talks, and there was always the hope the war would end before the situation exploded.

However, events came sharply to a head on 7th May, when the Commandant was seized by prisoners of one compound, who then bargained for his release. They demanded permission to form a Communist organization openly, with communication facilities and vehicles, and that there be no more 'forced screening'. The prisoners generally flared into open defiance and flew Communist flags. Some of the demands were agreed to, and on the 10th the Commandant was released. At this time there were about 163,000 prisoners held on Koje, in compounds each containing about 6,000. This agreement was repudiated by General Clark, who had just taken over from General Ridgway, and the Communists made considerable propaganda capital as a result.

On 10th June, using tear gas and concussion grenades, US paratroops moved into the compound to restore control, and although no firearms were used, one US soldier was killed and 14 wounded. During this incident, prisoners fought amongst themselves to prevent defectors coming over to the UN side, as well as against the troops restoring order, and 31 were killed and 139 wounded. Needless to say, the Communists drew world attention to the 'brutalities' of UN soldiers. About half the prisoners were moved to other islands, and those remaining on Koje were re-housed in smaller compounds, each between 500 and 600 men. To try and break the channels of communication, the civilian population was removed from the island. Encouraged by the weakness of the UN authorities in handling this incident, the prisoners on Koje, most of whom were under active Communist control and influence, remained a source of trouble, rioting and creating disturbances for propaganda purposes.

Rule by terror in the prison camps enabled the Communists to continue to use their 'sixth column', although not so efficiently, for the remainder of the 'negotiating war'. For example, on 14th December there was a mass demonstration in the Pongam Island camp, and when US troops moved in to restore authority, 85 prisoners were killed and 113 wounded. Again, this was first-rate material for the Communist propaganda machine, and full use was made of it. There was hesitation on the part of the UN in dealing with the ringleaders, who never in fact stood trial, for it was always hoped the war would be swiftly terminated and the whole unpleasant business forgotten.

On 13th July the UN announced the results of screening prisoners. Out of a total of about 112,000 soldiers and civilians held in UN prison camps so far screened, only 76,000 demanded to be sent home again. Of the approximately 20,000 Chinese 'volunteers', only 6,400 wanted to return to China. This was a bitter blow for the Communists, and one of the few UN Psychological successes of the war. Concurrently with this, there happened another UN success when anti-Communist civilians, who had been regarded as security risks, were being released. About 27,000 were freed during June, July and August in an operation known as 'Home Coming'. The howls of Communist protest at this measure indicated its effectiveness. More screening enabled a further 11,000 to be freed in October and November. They were removed from the clutches of the Communist prison camp organization that wished to terrorize and indoctrinate them. (On the other side of the line, the Communists had already used this tactic to their own advantage, when the previous autumn (1951) they released about 50,000

South Korean prisoners, immediately conscripting them into the KPA.)

Although a few UN prisoners were taken by the Communists in the summer of 1950, it was not until late autumn that rough camps were established. These eventually developed into two clusters, one around Pyongyang, which was transit and penal, and the other nearer the Yalu River, which was more permanent. These prison camps were deliberately situated near military targets, and while the Communists would not reveal their exact locations, they protested loudly to the world about UN inhumanities when they were bombed by UN aircraft. The treatment of UN and ROK prisoners was callous and barbaric, often extremely so. They had to make forced marches in winter and little shelter was provided, the prisoners having to fend largely for themselves, improvising both housing and clothing. There was no medical treatment at all for nine months, and after that medical aid was always scanty. Men suffered from such diseases as typhus and many died of neglect, malnutrition and starvation, since their rations were extremely inadequate.

The Communists made certain there was no chance of a UN 'sixth column' developing in the prison camps. As batches of prisoners were taken they were all herded closely together and left largely to their own devices for three days, during which time they were carefully watched. The natural leaders who possessed initiative above the average unconsciously asserted their qualities, and these usually amounted to 5 per cent of the total. They were removed to separate detention camps to be closely guarded, and were often placed in solitary confinement. These separated 'leaders' had a tough time, being beaten and often tortured, although if they were thought to be responsive, some were given special treatment in an effort to convert them to Communism.

The remainder, the 95 per cent, were left to themselves in camps in large groups, to starve, sink or swim, under only a light guard. Despite this and the fact there were anti-Communist guerrillas in the hills and that facilities for escape were, or could have been, engineered by the UN forces which had control of the air and the sea and possessed fleets of small craft able to land practically anywhere along the coast during darkness there are no recorded attempts of mass escapes, or even of groups getting away. The sad fact is that the bulk of the prisoners held by the Communists accepted their temporary fate without trying to alter it, and were little trouble to their captors, while those held by the UN banded themselves together into a virile, hostile and dangerous body.

From early 1951, the Communists tried to convert prisoners to their political creed, a procedure that achieved notoriety as 'brain washing', a phrase probably evolved from the colloquial Chinese 'Hsi Nao', which literally means 'to wash brain'. The Communists called it 'thought reform', and although they did not have quite as much success as is usually credited to them in this field, they made some notable conversions. The process consisted of lectures and continuous, monotonous, single-minded repetition. The object was first of all to destroy existing beliefs and ideals, and then to implant others in their place. The Communists insisted that South Korea started the war, for example, and that the USA was double-crossing its allies and was being double-crossed by them in the greed for world power and domination. Effects varied, but generally the prisoners remained mentally passive and co-operated no more than it was to their material benefit to do so.

Realizing that this method gained little lasting result and was a failure, the Communists, in mid-1952, changed to 'Voluntary study' groups, led by 'progressives', who were the converted, or at least ostensibly converted. A system of rewards for 'improved thoughts' and punishment for backward ones was employed. When prisoners were eventually repatriated, it was noticeable that some were less starved than others. Special efforts and enticements were made to try and obtain the co-operation of important prisoners, such as air force pilots, and especially to extract 'confessions'.

It is often wrongly alleged that there was a complete moral breakdown of UN personnel in the prison camps. The fact is that about 13 per cent went over to Communism, or overtly said they did, and this number was about equally divided between the weak and the opportunists. Perhaps one-third co-operated reluctantly with their captors to some degree, but those who criticize should consider the appallingly adverse conditions. Medical treatment, for example, was a bait for conversion and co-operation, and it was also alleged that some prisoners were used for medical experiments. The majority wanted simply to stay alive and to keep out of trouble. They did as they were told, and no more. Of the intellectuals, a few took to the study of the works of Mao Tse-tung, and became genuinely influenced by Communism, one of whom was the British double-spy, George Blake.[1] About 40 UN prisoners returned home convinced Communists, some singing 'The Internationale' and chanting Communist slogans while being repatriated. Twenty American and one British soldier refused to return at all, but most of them have become disillusioned and have rather shamefacedly crept back to the West.

The deduction must be that in the face of extremely tough conditions endured by UN prisoners and their resulting low physical and mental resistance, the Communist techniques of 'brain washing', while they should not be underrated, had only indifferent success. This opinion is reinforced by the fact that General Mark Clark estimated that during the war some 29,815 people had been killed by the Communists while in prison camps, of whom some 11,622 were UN and South Korean military personnel. In view of the atmosphere of terror this must have generated, much too much credit is given to the Communists in this sphere. Their success ratio of 13 per cent, if it was in reality as high as that since many alleged converts were simply opportunists, was small under the prevailing conditions.

One of the principal Communist propaganda tactics was the allegation that America was using germ warfare, and this obtained wide credence, especially as there were several severe epidemics during the war. It began in May 1951, when the

[1] George Blake was later sentenced to 42 years' imprisonment by a British court but escaped in 1966.

North Korean Foreign Minister alleged that the USA was deliberately spreading smallpox germs in his country, and in the following month China demanded that the Americans stop using bacteriological warfare methods. Little more was heard of this until February (1952), when the Communists on the Moscow radio accused America of poisoning wells, spreading smallpox and typhus bacteria and sending lepers into North Korea. This was widely echoed by both China and North Korea, which added that US airmen were dropping germ-laden rats over the country. In the winter of 1951–2, there were large scale typhus, smallpox, influenza and other epidemics raging because of a breakdown of the basic medical services. To lend substance to these allegations, many faked photographs were issued and faithfully reproduced by the Communist and sympathetic Press all over the world. 'Exhibits' were put on show in Peking.

The highlight came in May 1952, when two US airmen, who were prisoners, 'confessed' to dropping 'explosive germ bombs' over North Korea in the previous January. Other later 'confessions' of involvement in germ warfare were obtained from a few other UN prisoners, and a mass, show-piece trial was arranged. This was dropped in March 1953, when the Communists were frightened into agreeing to an armistice. At one time the propaganda was so great in volume that it was thought possibly to be a prelude to the Communists themselves embarking on this form of warfare. The success of this Communist propaganda was so great that even today, despite ample evidence to the contrary, many who are not Communists firmly believe that germ warfare was waged by the Americans in the Korean War.

Communist Parties in countries all over the world were willing helpers in the psychological war, faithfully repeating, often with embellishment, the charges and allegations against the UN and the USA by the Chinese and North Korean Governments. Using all means at their disposal they organized protest demonstrations and tried to influence public opinion in their favour. A few Western Communist newspaper correspondents were accredited to the Communist Forces in Korea, and they dutifully absorbed the hand-outs, sending back a stream of slanted copy. Doubts about the competence of UN leadership and quarrels between politicians and commanders were reported, omissions and faults were magnified or manufactured for the sole purpose of creating a lack of confidence in the UN Command.

There were also a great many 'do gooders', often genuine humanitarians, who were skilfully used by the Communists to further their cause. These people agitated against the war in Korea, took prominent parts in protest demonstrations and organized 'Bring our Boys Back Home' campaigns. For instance, when the Suiho Hydro Dam was first bombed in June 1952, there was a loud outcry from the British Labour Party and sections of the British Press condemned it. All this was bad for the morale of the fighting man in the combat zone, who felt that his country was not fully behind him, and for his family at home—which was just as the Communists intended it to be.

A brief comment on some of the methods and mediums used in the psychological war. The most obvious material for the Communists to work upon were the refugees, since up to three million fled south rather than remain under a Communist régime. Communist agents were planted among them to stir up discontent and start distressing rumours. Owing to the efficiency of the ROK security police and the general disinclination of the people towards Communism, this policy had an extremely limited success.

Many millions of leaflets were dropped by UN aircraft to the Communist forces during the war, urging them to give themselves up, offering safe conduct and casting doubts on the purity of their leaders' war aims. Their success can be measured to some extent by the fact that Communist soldiers were punished for simply picking up a UN leaflet, let alone for being caught reading one, or having a safe-conduct pass in the pocket. Leaflets were also aimed at civilians, who were not evacuated but had to remain at their jobs regardless of aerial bombardment, and one of the most telling warned them that at a certain time and date their installation or factory would be hit. This caused resentment at their own Government for not being able to prevent this taking place, and seriously affected civilian morale. At times leaflets dropped from the air were supplemented by 'voice aircraft', in which messages were broadcast by loud speaker to those on the ground. It had the advantage that the message got through to all within earshot, and there was nothing the Communists could do to prevent this, except improve their air defences and hustle their men underground.

The radio war, in which both sides took part, was used extensively from the beginning, the Communists continually making allegations and the UN constantly refuting them. The Communists made it an offence for anyone to listen to UN broadcasts. The effectiveness of the UN efforts tended to be limited as there were fewer radio sets available in North Korea, and the era of the transistor had hardly dawned. When the MLR stabilized, what could be called a 'loud speaker' war developed, each side broadcasting to the other across the narrow strip of 'no-man's-land', urging surrender, and alternately jeering and appealing. Accusations and smears were frequently made, and false news given out.

Both the North and South Korean authorities gave cash rewards for certain accomplishments and deeds, such as taking a feature, killing an enemy commander in battle, capturing an enemy personality or seizing new types of enemy weapons. This had spasmodic success on both sides, because to poorly paid soldiers, even Communist ones, a cash reward was attractive. The UN did not use these tactics until April 1953, when it offered $100,000 and political asylum for the first pilot to bring a MiG-15 intact over to the UN lines, and $50,000 for every succeeding one. Leaflets were dropped to spread this message, and the immediate reaction was for the Communists to ground all their MiGs for eight days, during which they presumably re-screened and re-indoctrinated the pilots. But it was not until the Armistice had been signed that a Communist pilot landed a MiG-15 in UN territory in September (1953), after which the cash offer was withdrawn. The Communists had a similar previous success, when a ROK pilot flew a light aircraft from the Kwanju air training centre in December 1952, where ROK pilots had been training to fly aircraft for some months, to North Korea. This resulted in a strict re-screening of ROK trainees.

There was a certain amount of guerrilla activity behind the lines on both sides, but its scope was limited and the character of the war tended to overshadow it. Details of anti-Communist guerrillas have not been revealed for the simple reason that retribution would be extracted from individuals concerned, or their families, in the customary Communist manner; but it was apparent that a guerrilla organization existed and was in contact with the UN Command. Its scope seems to have been limited to rescuing airmen who baled out from hit aircraft, and smuggling them down the coast where they were picked up by small craft of the UN navies. These anti-Communist guerrillas undertook practically no offensive action and concentrated upon staying alive in groups in the mountains. But as they were a threat and had nuisance value, during the winter of 1951–2 the Communists began a campaign against them, that included military action supplemented by promises and threats. It had little effect. Presumably it was UN Command policy not to activate the anti-Communist guerrillas, lest this invite their destruction, but to keep them in existence as an escape organization and for intelligence purposes.

Two comments seem obvious. First, why were UN personnel not snatched from prison camps? Second, why were Nationalist Chinese troops not used to reinforce the guerrillas?

Operating in the mountains in eastern Korea behind the UN lines were several thousand Communist guerrillas; no one seems to be sure exactly how many. At times they became bold, descending from the hills to pillage, ambush trucks and raid villages; but in early 1951 a US Marine division, with ROK support, mounted a fairly successful campaign that caused them to withdraw sharply farther into the security of the mountains. A further operation, known as 'Rat-killer', was mounted against them by two ROK divisions. This lasted from November

1951 to January 1952, and it was claimed that 26,000 guerrillas and bandits were eliminated. After this the Communist guerrillas remained more passive, being used primarily in an intelligence and sabotage role. They were fully under Communist control, but did not take the offensive, perhaps because this would have invited their elimination once the line stabilized. It is a little surprising that Communist China, with its tradition of guerrilla fighting, did not develop this form of warfare more fully, but perhaps the Soviet Military Mission, which had a diametrically opposite view about the value of guerrillas, pronounced decisively against such a policy.

In the psychological war the Communists generally had more success than the UN Command, and proof of this is that even today many in the West either still believe their allegations or suspect that there might be some truth in them. That the UN also had a certain success was demonstrated when large numbers of prisoners refused to return home, especially the Chinese 'volunteers'. A point that should be emphasized was that the Communists did less well than was realized in their 'brain washing' techniques.

The lesson that seems to stand out is that psychological warfare should be given a far greater priority than it now has in Western military study and training. All soldiers should understand its implications, be conditioned to play their part and be taught how to resist its pressures.

CHAPTER 11

In Retrospect

In looking back at the war in Korea, the first question to consider is—who won, and who gained what? At best a truce is a compromise, and in this case it enabled both sides to claim partial victory and various other gains. The fact is that from a shooting point of view the war bogged down into a deadly stalemate, which neither side, using conventional weapons, could have successfully broken. All the loss of life, suffering and expended material had been to little practical effect for the *de facto* border between North and South Korea remained much as it was before, in the region of the 38th Parallel. One thing the war did was to ensure, certainly for a generation at least, that the two parts of the country would never be united by democratic elections, as both the Communists and the West had hoped, although each upheld a differing interpretation of the word 'democratic'.

It was a war that neither side wanted. For the West, apprehensive of Soviet intentions in Europe, it was in the wrong place at the wrong time. For the Chinese it might have provoked massive retaliation before they had had time to put their own recently acquired house in order. The West claimed that it had been worthwhile because it had showed a determination to resist Communist aggression no matter where, by force of arms if necessary. If the UN had not stepped promptly in South Korea would have fallen, thus setting a precedent that would inevitably have resulted in many other small Asian countries being swallowed up in turn. It was a price that had to be paid to keep part of the world free. The Communists claimed that they had held at bay the superior armed might of the West, and had proved that an Asian army, even with inferior armaments, was a match for a combined Western one. In the psychological war they claimed complete victory.

It was the possession of atomic bombs by America, and the possible intention to use them, which brought about the Armistice, not the conventional military operations in which UN fire power was counterbalanced to a large extent by Communist manpower. This was possibly the only time that nuclear weapons could have been used without causing World War III. The Communists probably knew this but the West was not so sure.

Communist techniques were revealed to the world with clarity and they are being repeated today in Vietnam. The Communist aim is simple—to further its creed and power by any means available, including force. No deceit, intrigue or deception is scorned, but all are employed as and when they are considered capable of bringing some advantage to the Communists, or confusion to the West. A Communist may retreat, he may bargain, he may bend with a strong wind or he may temporarily compromise, but it will only be to gain time, to preserve his forces intact, to gain a respite or to carry out a stratagem. He is as faithful to the creed of Marx, Lenin and (if he is Chinese additionally to) Mao Tse-tung, as was any early Christian in the face of persecution.

If this premise is appreciated, Communist behaviour during the war becomes more comprehensible. At first, the Communists expected a swift victory over South Korea to be a *fait accompli* before either America or the UN woke up to the fact. They expected America to be too immersed in the Cold War with the Soviet Union to assist Korea. They miscalculated; but they were not dismayed and when the UN forces, after initial setbacks invaded and occupied most of North Korea, the next step was taken. Chinese 'volunteers' were flung into action by the hundred thousand. This was done because the Chinese calculated that America would not allow the Chinese Nationalists to attack the Chinese mainland, and so reopen the civil war, or to participate in the Korean fighting. More important still, they knew that America was going to limit her military aggression to the Korean peninsula and that atomic bombs were not going to be used. Had this not been the case, China, still tottering and weak, would not have entered the war against the UN.

When after some months the CPVA, beaten to its knees by UN fire power and about to be disastrously routed, became completely incapable of preventing most of North Korea from being reoccupied by UN forces, another Communist manoeuvre was tried. Without any real intention of making peace, but merely to gain respite for the CPVA, and knowing the mood of the UN countries, the Communists proposed truce negotiations. The UN agreed to halt its armies, thus allowing the beaten Communist forces to stabilize a fortified line across the peninsula. With the object of sapping as much UN strength and energy as possible, the Communists dragged out negotiations, employing every tactic in the psychological warfare book. These negotiations might still have been going on today, but for the fact that the Communists believed the Americans were fast losing patience and were about to use atomic bombs and carry the war to the Chinese mainland.

During the whole period of the war, the Communists, mainly the Chinese ones, never deviated from their ultimate aim, never showed any sign of humanity, never gave an inch unless compelled to do so by force or fear and took all concessions for weaknesses to be exploited to the full. It was clearly demonstrated in Korea, from 1950 until 1953, how the Communists wage war.

The Korean War has frequently been described as a 'limited' one, but this is only partly correct. It was a limited one for the UN as voluntary limitations were accepted to prevent its spread outside the Korean Peninsula and for brief moments even north of the 38th Parallel; but it was certainly not limited on the Communist side, as the Chinese used all means they could. They recognized no limits except those enforced by UN fire power. If the Chinese had possessed atomic bombs, they would almost certainly have used them. The Soviet Union did not allow any atomic weapons to go to Korea, partly because it did not have many, but mainly because it feared the American nuclear strategy of total retaliation.

This poses the question of why the Communists began the war. The answer is simple. They began it because they thought they could win quickly and also to test Western reaction to aggression. Although there is lack of documentary proof, one feels that the instigator was Stalin, who carried Mao Tse-tung and the Chinese people along with him for his own purposes. The promptitude with which members of the UN joined together against the Communists must have startled him, but he continued to push as far forward as possible as ruthlessly as was necessary.

This was the first time that the UN showed its teeth and the fact that a UN army materialized in Korea must have given the Communists cause for reconsideration. Although of doubtful legality, since South Korea was not even a member, UN intervention was swift. The weight of the burden of the fighting devolved on American and ROK troops, and without American fighting men and material aid the war in Korea could not have been waged for very long.

Most of the UN contingents, with the exception of the Commonwealth and Turkish, were only token ones. These small detachments from many nations provided the façade of UN unity, but were of doubtful value in many instances because of their small size. Several nations have been criticized for not sending larger contingents as most of them could well have done, except perhaps France, which was fully engaged in Indo-China. Even the Commonwealth has been criticized for only producing a division, and the Turks a brigade, but the answer was that Britain had many other military commitments, and the Turkish Army was required to support a weak flank in the Cold War. In round figures, there were eventually about 35,000 UN troops, exclusive of US ones, of which 20,000 were Commonwealth and 5,000 Turkish, fighting in Korea.

As may be guessed, these small contingents varied considerably in standards of training and battle techniques. A UN reception centre was set up to clothe and equip them as they arrived and all were given US arms, uniforms and equipment. A course on familiarization with American weapons and tactics was carried out which enabled their proficiency to be evaluated. More to the point, these national contingents were of varying combat ability, and some had to be assigned to quieter sectors for obvious reasons. They also posed problems arising from languages, customs and food, but these were overcome by improvising and compromising. For example, only the Canadian, Norwegian and Swedish troops took the full US rations as issued; all the others had to have them modified in some way to suit national tastes.

Little need be said about the combat ability and morale of the Commonwealth troops. They were universally recognized as admirable. Those of the Turks, who had not seen active service for many years, were also very high. A comment might however be made on those of the American ground troops, which have been reported sometimes as splendid and sometimes as doubtful. The fact is that both descriptions could be applied at different times. In the early days of the war, after soft living in Japan, the American soldier did not always contrast favourably with the hardy Korean fighting man. It was found that the policy of giving pep talks on the aims, good intentions and righteousness of the UN cause, did little to produce results.

When General Ridgway took over the 8th Army at a critical juncture, he changed all this, maintaining that toughness, skill at arms and a determination to get in and win the fight was the best way to raise morale. He was right. Confident, capable soldiers generate high morale and he quickly swept away traces of depression and defeatism. Under his command the American combat soldier blossomed out and for the remainder of the war his conduct in battle was of an exceedingly high standard. It was later alleged, when the line stabilized, that the comforts and sophisticated way of living 'softened' US troops, but this was not the case by any means, as anyone, such as myself, who has often seen them in action, can testify. In mobile warfare the American soldier was in every way superior to the Communist one, and in the later positional battles I saw no reason to reverse this opinion.

That the war in Korea was unpopular in many quarters in America was bound to some extent to affect the morale of the fighting men in action. The psychological success of the Communists in marshalling sections of world opinion against them also had some small effect. But despite these handicaps the spirit and cheerfulness of American soldiers remained amazingly high. A rotation system operated enabling a man to return home after a combat tour of between nine and twelve months, and also during his service in Korea he was flown at least once to Japan for a short recreational leave. The war in Korea brought about the integration of negro soldiers in the US armed forces, with excellent results, the coloured men fighting extremely well alongside white comrades. Previously, negro soldiers had been in separate units, some of which had not done so well in World War II, and even in early days in Korea. At first the integration had been a temporary expedient, necessitated by units being broken up in battle and consequent shortages of manpower, but it worked so well that the principle was established and the rules changed. Its advantages are seen today in Vietnam.

Often much maligned and neglected were the troops of the ROK, which provided the largest ground combat element, exceeding even that of the USA. The ROK forces had many handicaps: inferior weapons, no armour, little artillery, hardly any transport, low pay. Yet, despite these drawbacks, on the whole they fought very well. The build-up of the ROK forces was deliberately retarded, partly for political reasons, the Americans not wishing an armed force to develop that might be capable of independent aggression, partly because there was a shortage of equipment, and partly because there was the suspicion that they were unreliable in action. The official reason was that the ROK forces could not be expanded rapidly until more South Korean officers were trained, and it was not until late 1952 that this policy was modified. In early days US divisions were very glad to take in large numbers of ROK semi-trained men (KATUSAs) to fill their ranks, and these became very good combat soldiers at squad level. Many US divisions had eventually up to 2,500 integrated into units, without whom they would have been much under strength. Largely because of the good performance put up by the KATUSAs in battle, early opinions of them were often revised.

General Van Fleet appreciated the fact that the South Koreans were good fighting material, and he established training centres, staffed by US personnel, to give combat training. From this time onwards there was lessening resistance to Syngman Rhee's demands for more facilities to increase his ROK army. The US Advisers of KMAG (Korean Military Advisory Group), who were attached to ROK formations and units, supported this new view, speaking in most instances very highly of the men they were with.

A few ROK divisions had somehow remained intact, being continually in the forefront of the attack or defence, usually in the hilly, barren country in the eastern part of the peninsula. By June 1951 there were ten ROK divisions, which were gradually taking on a larger share of the fighting, but they were basically infantry. These had increased to 16 by the time of the Armistice, when they had assumed responsibility for about 75 per cent of the MLR. The ROK divisions were less well equipped than those of the US, and the Americans were reluctant to put sophisticated arms and material into unskilled hands. Lack of education was given as a reason for not training more skilled technicians. It was probably because of this that in the latter stages of the war the Communists singled them out as targets. And it was probably because they did not have enough artillery and other support weapons that they gave way on occasions under the weight of concentrated Communist punches.

Generally, the ROK Army had ample manpower, but lacked experienced officers. The senior officers were all young for the rank they held, and as most were Japanese-trained, the army developed some Japanese techniques and customs. All, both officers and men, were loyal to Syngman Rhee, and he could, and did, at times personally issue orders to them that were not in keeping with UN policy. These were instantly obeyed without question. The ROK military personnel were first and foremost Koreans, fighting for their country, and while being grateful for UN aid, had reservations about some aspects of its policy. Practically all the ROK troops were southerners, with parochial views about those from the northern part of their country, and the defection rate was small. In the first advances the Communists had stamped out any potential or latent sympathy the southerners might have had or developed.

ROK troops had fairly elementary rations, living mainly on fish and rice, and throughout the war had supply problems. Many units ran businesses, such as fishing, and sold their produce to other units and the civilian population, using the money to supplement their rations. Syngman Rhee wanted the US to be responsible for providing his army with food, but this was not agreed to for political and economic reasons. The ROK troops always complained that the Communist prisoners of war were better fed than they, which was true. The conscript labour Korean Service Corps, that worked for the UN forces in the field, was fed by a special arrangement, but did not, as it would have liked, have full UN rations. The result was that a well-fed, well-equipped and well-supported US division would fight alongside a ROK one that was poorly fed and less well equipped and supported, but was expected to do the same job, and was criticized patronizingly if it failed.

After being virtually destroyed in 1950, the Korean People's Army, the KPA, was gradually reconstituted and expanded, until by the end of the war it consisted of three corps. It was a Communist-type force, firmly conditioned and controlled by commissars, and it became an efficient one. Lieutenant-General Nam Il, the Chief of Staff, who had been a captain in the Soviet Army in World War II, was an able military leader, as well as a shrewd political manipulator. In general the North Koreans fought better than the South Koreans, against whom they were mainly matched, the will to triumph being more deeply instilled by Communist practice and teaching.

The pitching of North Korean soldiers against those from the south was deliberate, since civil wars are notoriously more lastingly bitter than international ones. Calculated psychological action was taken by the Communists to ensure that there would be no collusion with troops on the other side, either at the time or for a generation ahead. The country is now solidly divided ideologically.

For the first time in modern history large Chinese armies clashed with Western forces on the battlefield, and such is the quality of Communist propaganda that many in the West firmly believe that the Chinese won hands down and that accordingly it would be folly to tangle with them in the future. This is nonsense. A million of the best Chinese soldiers were hopelessly defeated within eight months, by about one-third that number of UN troops. Skill and fire power outclassed the best fighting men that China, after decades of war, could produce.

Being a reliable Communist, dedicated to Mao Tse-tung's interpretation of Marx, was a prime requirement for both commanders and men. The best Communists do not always make the best soldiers, and individual military efficiency was often low. Later this improved as experience was gained by corps and divisional commanders the hard way. Also, General Peng removed some of the more incompetent, and generally military efficiency improved with battle experience, but it never rose to the heights claimed for it by Communist propaganda. Ample evidence is available that the Chinese soldiers were not volunteers, but were picked regulars from the Field Armies on the mainland. From the time CPVA armies entered Korea until General Peng came on the scene, there was confusion and muddle, despite the achievements of large scale movement by night and good camouflage. A capable general, he established order and system, but nevertheless it was not the orderliness one would expect to see in a well organized and controlled Western expeditionary force. Working by rule of thumb and under the threat of the commissar and unit political officer, the CPVA creaked along clumsily.

Troop training standards were low compared with Western ones. The so-called 'mass' tactics were simply the result of poorly trained troops instinctively huddling together, a fault Western armies try to eradicate early in recruit training. Lack of adequate communications contributed to the density of troops to space in the field, while the Communist disregard for human life forced the unfortunate soldiers yet closer together in the assault, as they were projected at UN strongpoints. The 'mass assault', the 'human sea', was simply an expedient. The Communists made a virtue of necessity.

Motivation was instilled by indoctrination within the CPVA, where there was rigid political control at all levels. Orders were never questioned and accordingly lower leadership was poor. Individual reaction was rare, and initiative rarer. Much has been made of the so-called fanatical bravery of the Chinese soldiers. It is true that they were all psychologically conditioned for battle, and that they feared their commissars more than the enemy, but it is also true that at times they were afraid, faltered, ran away, panicked, deserted, gave themselves up and defected. These traits and tendencies, natural in an indifferently trained army, seem to have been largely overlooked. In mobile warfare the CPVA was outclassed, being beaten to a standstill; but when the line stabilized it came into its own, as each assault could be carefully planned and rehearsed until each man knew his part before being launched.

Massive participation by the Chinese brings into question the extent of Soviet influence. The North Korean Army was trained and comparatively well equipped by the Soviet Union, and the huge number of jet aircraft, guns, armoured vehicles, trucks and weapons used by the Chinese were provided by Russia. Soviet instructors and technicians taught the Chinese how to use the equipment and arms, and for a time Soviet pilots even flew some of the MiG-15 jets over North Korea. Large credits and other aid were granted to China to enable it to fight the war. In view of this it must be assumed that throughout Soviet influence on its conduct must have been great, despite an increasing Chinese say in its direction.

A large Soviet Military Mission in North Korea prepared the plans, and carried out much of the staff work essential to move and feed such huge numbers, but Soviet personnel kept in the background, allowing the impression to be formed that the prosecution of the war had become mainly a Chinese responsibility. Without Soviet material aid and Soviet military staff assistance, the war could not have been fought, and Soviet influence was such that Stalin could have stopped it overnight had he wished to do so. It was not until after his death that this influence changed to some degree, and the Chinese were able to assume a paramount position. It is of interest that the Chinese did not agree to a truce until after Stalin's death, though for some months previously there had been a distinct possibility that the US might be provoked into using atomic bombs.

Hovering in the background throughout the war were some 500,000 Nationalist Chinese troops waiting on Formosa to reopen the civil war. They were not used, even though at one stage the UN was desperately short of manpower, and the US 7th Fleet patrolled the Straits of Formosa to ensure that they did not assault the mainland on their own initiative. General MacArthur was latterly prepared to use them, as was General Mark Clark, had they been permitted to do so, and the point is often raised of why were they not employed; and, if they had been committed, what would have been the outcome.

Despite conflicting reports on their capability, the Nationalist Chinese troops were undoubtedly better trained and equipped than any in the CPVA. Had they been flung into Korea it is possible that the Communists might have been decisively defeated in battle within six months or sooner.

The reasons why they were not used were twofold. Use of Chiang Kai-shek's troops would have reopened the civil war and the American Administration, full of distaste for the conflict in Korea, wanted to pull out at the first opportunity. If the

Chinese civil war had been reopened there was a danger that the US might have become deeply and almost indefinitely involved in the Far East. At that time, with Stalin poised in Europe, this argument was undoubtedly correct. The other reason was that President Syngman Rhee flatly refused to have Nationalist Chinese forces in his country, since he did not want it to become another perpetually devastated cockpit of Chinese armed conflict. He was single-minded in his objection; and he just as firmly rejected General Mark Clark's suggestion that two Nationalist Chinese divisions be included in the UN Command. In retrospect, the decision not to use Chiang Kai-shek's soldiers at any stage remains a controversial one. The factors on each side are obvious and difficult to weigh against each other.

On the more technical aspects of the war, air power demands first attention. A tremendous aerial effort was put into the conflict by America, and there was a school of thought convinced that air power could successfully finish the war. The UN air forces had control of the air and were able to pound Communist installations as they wished; but despite the rain of bombs, rockets and napalm on North Korea, supplies still reached the front line, and the life of the country continued. Escalation was slow, since there was a reluctance to destroy targets like the major dams, which if attacked earlier would have made the Communist supply problems more acute. The reason for hesitation was the hope that the Communists would realize they were beaten and come to the conference table quickly; while the undamaged facilities were there, normal services could be restored to the people in reasonable time. The lesson to be emphasized—one not fully absorbed in World War II—is that air power alone cannot force a military decision on a determined enemy. A similar problem is presenting itself in Vietnam. But one should not underrate air power, as without aerial pressure the Communists would have been able to prosecute the war more vigorously and more easily. Strategic bombing and interdiction slowed down and hampered the enemy considerably, disrupting and disorganizing. Aerial

interdiction and close ground support saved the Pusan Perimeter at a critical moment, and vitally assisted the UN forces
throughout the war. Had it not been for self-imposed limitations, UN air power might have achieved greater results. If
aircraft had been allowed to cross the Yalu River to attack
installations, industrial complexes, concentration and training
areas and airfields, it would have made the task of the Communists very much harder, and that of the UN Command very
much easier.

The Korean War saw the first clashes between jet aircraft,
when Communist MiG-15s battled with F-86s (Sabre Jets). It
is estimated that in all the Chinese, and North Koreans,
received some 4,000 jet planes from the Soviet Union, as well
as other types of aircraft. At the end of the war they had
between 1,600 and 2,000 aircraft of different types in service.
UN pilots were superior to Communist ones, and in the
fighting in MiG Alley, about 850 MiGs were shot down for the
loss of only 58 F-86s. This accounted for the fact that the MiGs
never flew far from base, and when in the air herded together in
large groups. Communist air losses probably totalled about
2,800 in all. It is thought they lost about 1,400 in aerial combat;
that another 400, damaged in combat, crashed on the way
back to base; and that about 1,000 were lost because of
accidents and mechanical faults. The cost to the UN air forces
was higher, amounting to about 3,300 altogether, of which
about half were shot down, mainly by ground fire, and the
remainder lost because of accident or mechanical failure.

Little of interest emerged on the naval side of the war, which
began with an emphasis on amphibious operations, given to it
by the successful Inchon landing, but then changed to one of
blockade, bombardment and mine warfare. Warships of the
UN navies kept the Communists tightly within their land
confines. Amphibious operations indicate an offensive spirit
but, after initial forays, these were drastically reduced and then
stopped, except for undercover escape activities. The policy was
not to provoke the enemy since it was hoped that peace was
round the corner.

No new techniques evolved from the Korean War. Improved weapons were brought into service, while tactics were, as always, modified and adapted to the terrain and special circumstances. During the static period, little of theoretical value emerged that had not been illustrated in World War I.

The one new vehicle to emerge in Korea that may influence the future shape of tactics was the helicopter, soon to become the popular military work-horse. When the MLR stabilized, all casualties were evacuated instantly by helicopter and this was a great boost to the morale of the fighting forces of the UN. Today, used in its hundreds in Vietnam, its characteristics, advantages and drawbacks have been thoroughly examined; but service in Korea was in its early days, when its potentialities had yet to be discovered and tested. The first battle mission of helicopters, as far as it can be established (there are varying claims), was in January 1951, when they were used in the Seoul area to evacuate casualties. After this they became widely employed for this purpose and many hundreds of wounded UN soldiers who otherwise would have died were saved by them. Life-giving blood plasma was often administered in flight. On initial journeys to the forward zone to pick up casualties, the helicopters carried rations and ammunition. Both at sea and on land they were used to rescue pilots of downed aircraft. In October the same year (again there are conflicting claims), Marines were carried into battle near the Punch Bowl by helicopter, and the following month a whole battalion was lifted into the combat area. Techniques of medical evacuation, supply, troop carrying and rescue quickly improved.

The Korean War emphasized the democratic principle that the military commander must always be subordinate to his civilian political master, and this was demonstrated when Truman dismissed MacArthur. This episode demonstrated, too, that in modern warfare a general must win within the terms of his political brief.

Finally, the UN humanitarian efforts deserve a mention, UNCACK (UN Civil Assistance Command, Korea) was formed to provide relief for the civilian population, sections of which were in dire need of many essentials. To the war-ravaged people of South Korea and their problems were added some three million destitute refugees from the north. UNCACK distributed food, clothing, helped to provide shelter and to reconstruct communications and other civil facilities.

While the war in Korea may have been a mere side-show, it momentarily stemmed the Communist tide and was a reasonably successful outpost campaign. It was worth fighting and UN soldiers did not die in vain. Had it not been fought, South Vietnam would have fallen in 1955. A massed Communist-style infantry advance over the land frontier would have almost certainly been attempted, had there not been a 'Korean precedent' to show that such a move would instantly provoke US and UN armed retaliation. Instead, in South Vietnam, the Communists had to revert to Mao Tse-tung's old, slow method of guerrilla infiltration—a long, tedious, wearying process, and nowadays by no means such a sure one. The Communists would rather have a swift, conventional victory, than spend expensive and immensely exhausting years on guerrilla warfare. The war in Korea showed them that there was no safe alternative.

Appendix A

UN Contribution in Korea

Of the fifty-three nations that endorsed the UN decision to take action in Korea against the Communist aggressors, only sixteen provided combat elements, while another five provided medical units. South Korea was not a member of the UN, and so is not mentioned, nor is America, as its contribution has been covered in the text.

UN countries contributed armed forces as shown:

Australia	—*Two infantry battalions, naval forces and a squadron of aircraft
Belgium	— One infantry battalion
Canada	— *An infantry brigade, including artillery and armoured elements, and a squadron of aircraft
Colombia	— One infantry battalion and one warship
Ethiopia	— One infantry battalion
France	— One infantry battalion
Greece	— One infantry battalion and transport aircraft
Luxembourg	— One infantry company
Netherlands	— One infantry battalion and warships
New Zealand	—*A regiment of artillery
Philippines	— One infantry battalion and an armoured company
Thailand	— One infantry battalion, warships and aircraft
Turkey	— One infantry brigade
Union of South Africa	— One aircraft squadron
United Kingdom	—*Three infantry brigades, one armoured brigade, artillery, engineer and supporting ground forces, warships and aircraft squadrons.

*Most of these units were merged into the 1st Commonwealth Division when it was formed in July 1951.

Appendix A

UN countries sending Medical Units were:

Denmark
India
Italy
Norway
Sweden.

Appendix B

List of Published Sources

The following works have been consulted in compiling this book, and grateful acknowledgment is made to the authors, contributors, reporters and publishers.

Appleman, Roy E. *South to the Naktong*. US Department of the Army Historical Division Publication (1961)

Barclay, C. N. *First Commonwealth Division*. Gale & Polden, Aldershot (1954)

Biderman, A. D. *March to Calumny*. Macmillan Company, New York (1963)

Cagle, M. W. and Manson, F. A. *The Sea War in Korea*. A US Naval Institute Publication (1957)

Chae-Gyong, O. *Handbook of Korea*. Pageant Press, New York (1958)

Clark, General Mark. *From the Danube to the Yalu*. Harrap, London (1954)

Deane, P. *Captive in Korea*. Hamish Hamilton, London (1953)

Eisenhower, Dwight D. *Mandate for Change, 1953-56*. Heinemann, London (1963)

Farrar-Hockley, A. *Edge of the Sword*. Muller, London (1954)

Futrell, Robert F. *US Air Force in Korea—1950-53*. Duell, Sloan & Pearce, New York (1961)

Geer, Andrew. *New Breed: The Story of the US Marines in Korea*. Harper Brothers, New York (1952)

Hunter, Edward. *Brain Washing in Red China*. Vanguard Press, New York (1951)

Joy, Charles Turner. *How Communists Negotiate*. Macmillan Company, New York (1955)

Kahn, E. J. *The Peculiar War*. Random House, New York (1952)

Karig, W. from official sources. *Battle Report.* Vol. 6, *War in Korea.* Holt, Rinehart, New York (1952)

MacArthur, Douglas. *Reminiscences.* Heinemann, London (1964)

Marshall, S. L. A. *The River and the Gauntlet.* William Morrow & Co., New York (1953)

Marshall, S. L. A. *Pork Chop Hill.* William Morrow & Co., New York (1956)

Marshall, S. L. A. *Military History of the Korean War.* F. Watts (1963)

Millis, Walter. *Arms and the State.* Twentieth Century Fund, New York (1958)

Politella, Darie. *Operation Grasshopper.* Robert R. Longo, Wichita (1958)

Rees, D. *Korea—The Limited War.* Macmillan, London (1964)

Rhee, Syngman. *Korea Flaming High* (Vols. 1-3). Korea Office of Public Information (1955-9)

Ridgway, General Matthew B. *The Korean War.* Doubleday, New York (1967)

Ridgway, General Matthew B. *Soldiers.* Harper, New York (1956)

Schien, Edgar H. and others. *Coercive Persuasion.* Norton & Co., New York (1961)

Spanier, J. W. *The Truman-MacArthur Controversy.* O.U.P. (1959)

Stewart, Colonel James T., editor. *Air Power.* Van Nostrand, Princeton (1957)

Truman, Harry S. *Years of Trial & Hope—1946-53*, Vol. 2. Hodder & Stoughton, London (1956)

Thompson, R. *Cry Korea.* Macdonald, London (1951)

Vather, W. H. *Panmunjon.* Stevens & Sons, London (1958)

Whiting, A. S. *China Crosses the Yalu.* Macmillan Company, New York (1960)

Worden, W. L. *General Dean's Story.* Weidenfeld & Nicolson, London (1954)

Korea—1950. US Department of the Army Publication (1952)

Korea—1951-53. US Department of the Army Publication (1956)

Index

The following words are not included in the Index as they appear on the majority of the pages of the book:

Formations

88025

O'BALLANCE, EDGAR
    KOREA, 1950-1953.

DATE DUE